Coaching Wisdom

Voices of the Gay Coaches Alliance

ISBN: 978-0-578-38214-2

DEDICATION

To GCA founders
Harry Faddis, Dave Allen, Michael Cohen, and Allen Siewert;

To Thomas Leonard,
founder and pioneer of professional coaching.; and

To the future success of the coaching profession
and to all members of the Gay Coaches Alliance.

CONTENTS

INTRODUCTION

INTRODUCTION

By Tim Kincaid

This book offers the unique perspectives of members of the international Gay Coaches Alliance (GCA), a professional organization for coaches who identify as gay men. There is scant information in academic publications or the popular press that focuses on gay men who are coaches and about coaching gay men. As coaches who identify as gay men, our unique take on life and the world deserves to be heard. We believe this book makes a contribution to knowledge, practice, and understanding for anyone interested in coaching, regardless of sexual orientation or gender identity.

This book is by and about men who identify as gay—the G in enormously diverse LGBTQ+ community. The intention of this book is about focus, not exclusion. We sincerely hope that this book inspires publications that focus on coaching and the unique needs of those who identify as LBTQ+. More broadly, we hope this book inspires needed research and writing about coaching in the context of diverse communities.

The genesis of the book was a suggestion in 2017 by GCA member (and chapter contributor) Jim Lopata at the annual International Gay Coaches Conference. Those gathered agreed that we knew of no other book that centered on coaching and gay men. The idea was intriguing, but it took two years of rumination before the time and energy finally came together for this project. A book editorial committee formed in 2019 and a call for contributions was met with about two dozen chapters submitted from GCA members all over the world.

Book Topics Explored

This book is an anthology of writing by GCA members about our experiences and perspectives that can offer new insights to the field of coaching and other helping professions. The authors provided chapters that were either anecdotal reflections or more in-depth articles in the realm of theory, application, and practice. Some of the questions our member/authors explore are:

- How does being a gay coach inform your practice working with clients?
- How does being a gay coach inform your practice working with non-gay clients
- How has working with a gay coach impacted your own life?
- What does the coaching community at large need to know about coaching gay men?
- What unique perspectives can you share with non-gay coaches and allied helping professionals?

Who this book is for?

We set out to create a book that would be interesting and useful for many audiences:

- Gay male coaches and other helping professionals (all experience levels)
- Non-gay coaches and other helping professionals who may work with gay men
- Gay men who want to learn more about how coaching might benefit them
- Gay men who are interested in becoming a coach
- Academia, including social science researchers, teachers, and counselors
- Professional coaching organizations, schools, and coaching trainers

Near the end of the book project, our belief that there is a need for this book was confirmed by a communication to the GCA president from a large university:

"I am the Curriculum Manager for the Health and Wellness Coaching Department at Maryland University of Integrative Health. I am contacting you in your role as president of the Gay Coaches Alliance. I am looking for an article, some blog posts, or similar material to offer our students as a resource to raise awareness related to coaching the LGBTQ+ community. I had little success with a Google search on the topic. I am hoping you might be able to point me to some available resources, or, if not, to someone else who might be able to help me. Thank you for considering this request."

Happily, we are able to share some book content now, before the book is released in May 2022, on the GCA website www.thegaycoaches.com.

We hope this book is the first to inspire research and writing about coaching and diverse communities.

FOREWARD

2

WHY THE "GAY" IN THE "GAY" COACHES ALLIANCE?"

By Harry Faddis

We've been asked this question many times and, indeed, we've often challenged ourselves with the same question. The inquiry breaks out into several sections:

- Why do we need a "gay" group of coaches?
- What do we possibly get from this association?
- What are the contributions that we make to the larger culture or the greater good?

The need for a gay alliance can be seen by a look at the general history of gay men as well as in conjunction with the Gay Coaches Alliance at its annual Conference at The Easton Mountain Retreat Center, where the GCA has found a hospitable environment for its work.

Gay men have not been living in an accepting culture for that many years. In the olden days, we were fearful and secretive. Like other sub-cultures, we had our own secret language, we gathered in our own secret places, and we developed the ability (gaydar) to recognize each other from a distance. When we wanted to signal to another that we were similar, we made a secret signal. This was called, "dropping a hair pin." When I met you, I might indicate my love for the theater. Innocent enough, but that clue might lead to further "hair pins." And when we talked among ourselves, we often referred to other gay men as "she." Not because we want to be feminized, but we wanted our conversation, if overheard, to appear to be us talking about a girlfriend. I might say, "What's she doing now?" when I was indicating a boyfriend. There are a large number of books about just this topic: gay men forming a sub-culture to survive, coming out and staying in, and finding our own Gay Myths.

At The Easton Mountain Retreat Center, where I live, we have been devoted to the healing of the souls of gay men for twenty years. We host many events for gay men. At one of these, a man shared this in a closing circle: "Now for the first time in my life, I know what straight men must feel walking through the world." This experience of complete and visceral belonging is something gay men need. One of the members of the Gay Coaches Alliance reported how he realized he belonged when he arrived at the Conference at Easton Mountain. He said that he finally felt at home when he saw a seven-foot drag queen coming out of the Drag Closet, just across the way from a hot tub holding a half dozen gay men.

As a sub-culture, gay men need to love and accept other gay men, that is, to recognize and heal our own internal homophobia. We need to be separate to do this; it's a principle of alchemy that separation of elements is prior to combination. This acceptance required us to address classism, racism, ageism, and sexism in our own group.

The Gay Coaches Alliance recognizes that we all have a need to be accepted and when this acceptance is present, we all can grow into our own kind of person and coach. From a positive community experience such as this, we all are lifted up. When I attended The Coaches Training Institute, I wondered where are all the gay men were. Except for a few of the trainers who were quietly gay, I rarely met another gay student. When I attended the first Coachville Conference with Thomas Leonard in Las Vegas in 2003, I had the occasion to introduce myself to the whole group of 800-plus coaches as a gay coach, and I was thereafter included in a posse of gay coaches. This is what we get from this association: camaraderie and mutual acceptance.

The mission of the Gay Coaches Alliance is to grow the number of gay coaches in the world, as well as to increase the number of gay men who become coaches. Most of us have the viewpoint that gay men have unique voices and gifts to bring to the world. Because of our various kinds of oppressions, we have grown up to have a different way of looking at reality, people, and the world. This is also true for people oppressed by gender, sex, race, and class. This difference gives many of us the ability to be compassionate and caring.

Not only do we have the exciting gifts of creativity in the arts, we also have the gifts of healing which we notice in the many places where we work such as in the hospital room and in children's classrooms. These gifts need to be nurtured and grown. What better way than to dot the land with ten thousand gay coaches, working in all places, boardrooms and prisons; youth centers and hospitals; kindergartens and campsites. In order for us to rise up in a generation, gay men need help, a lot of help. Many gay men in their forties and fifties are having the realization that they want to make a career change from the corporate world to the coaching world. These men need the help of coaches to navigate this challenging transition. We also need other kinds of help that includes coaching. In the last year, two men and GCA Members, Zach Bulls and Andrew Sartory, started a new organization called Gay Man Thriving. In their own words, their mission is: "We are fiercely committed to ending the loneliness epidemic in the gay male community, one man at a time."

Many young gay men are wanting to train to be coaches and need help—spiritual, emotional, and financial. Even now, there are generous gay coaches in the GCA offering pro bono coaching to young people in community centers in urban areas. Thomas Leonard, the father of coaching, held the viewpoint that: Everyone Is a Coach. He dreamed of a world where the way we relate to each other as coach and client would become an ordinary way of relating, just because it makes us all feel better, do better, and be better.

For the future, I see a world in which an organization for gay men is valuable. That is, an organization of old and young, of men of all colors and men of every class. We have often discussed opening the alliance up to others: to women and to queer-identified folk. Most of us learned in coaching school to be wary of either/or situations or forced choice scenarios. I propose the very useful and/and strategy. Let's have a coach alliance for gay men, and one for lesbians, and one for queer folk. Many members of the GCA would gladly join these groups and, indeed, be of service in helping them get established. Imagine a future conference that included fifty or a hundred members from each of these groups. Now, that would set the world aflame.

As the GCA continues to grow, we experience the coming and going of many members. So, the work of being faithful to our mission becomes more important as the years pass. We are always welcoming in new members who have joined us because of who we are—a "gay" alliance. This was true eighteen years ago and it is still true today. Our mission remains fresh. At our 10th GCA International Conference, April 30-May 1, 2021, we were blessed to welcome many new members from across the globe, made possible because of a virtual conference. This is the kind of growth we are reaching for: growth of nations, colors, ages, and classes.

Our membership in the GCA is now at 114. As one scrolls down the photos one cannot help but be amazed at the variety of all the faces and, as one reads the biographical information, one is even more struck by the diversity of the work that these gay coaches are doing. Imagine with me what this alliance will look like in five years and you'll be able to have some perspective about how these men will make meaningful contributions to the local and international communities. I hope you will be amazed and grateful, as I am, with the contributions of GCA Members in this book.

3

THE GAY COACHES ALLIANCE ORIGINS AND A BRIEF HISTORY

By Harry Faddis

One day in early May 2005, a group of gay men gathered in the corner library at The Easton Mountain Retreat Center and created what became The Gay Coaches Alliance. It was a happenstance grouping and came together because of something else. Perhaps one of us said something and then someone else said another thing and, quite easily, the question arose: Why don't we start a group of gay coaches? The men of this group were: Dave Allen, Michael Cohen, Alfred DePew, Joe Weston, and me. We followed the origin-pattern of many small non-profit groups: a few people sitting around figuring out how to bring something positive to the world and then someone has an idea. No one of us had this idea. We all did.

At that time, the thing to do was to make a website and then, so we thought, launch into a world of coaches just waiting to join. We enlisted our colleague Allen Siewert to design and manage our website and then we waited. Nothing happened in the following several years, except that we met on a semi-regular basis to discuss the profession of coaching and to encourage each other in our work.

At some point three of us gathered and decided to re-organize and to create a plan for growth. Two of our original members left the group and the remaining founders of the new group were Dave Allen, Michael Cohen, Allen Siewert, and me. The all-new website shared with the world our mission: to grow the number of gay men who became coaches and to increase the number of gay men who hired coaches. Embedded in the mission is to recognize that, as a group, gay men have an abundance of gifts that the world needs such as compassion, healing, and the perspective of an outsider. We need to have coaches in order to unleash these gifts among ourselves and to coach others into living up to their great potential.

We established the monthly calls for members and another for the business of the alliance. They began as telephone conference calls and evolved into Zoom calls a few years ago. We have been meeting monthly for the last sixteen years.

When I proposed that we have a conference, I had no idea of how to do it.

I was asked by my fellow coaches: Why do it? What's going to be the purpose? I remember confessing: I don't know why but I do know that something will happen when these men gather in one room and look around at each other. Something will surely happen and I know it will be interesting, dynamic, and inspirational. It will further our growth. Finally, we worked through some obstacles and decided to produce our first conference. We were greatly aided by two of our members, Tim Kincaid and Terry Hildebrandt, each of whom had a lot of experience attending conferences. Through their leadership we were able to make a start.

The real launching of The Gay Coaches Alliance came about through organizing the First Annual International Gay Coaches Conference, held at The Easton Mountain Retreat Center in upstate New York in the first week of May, 2010. At that time, we had about thirty members and most of these men attended this conference. We continued this annual conference until 2020, when we had our first virtual conference as a result of the pandemic.

At this first conference we met Garry Schleifer, the publisher of choice Magazine, the one and only magazine for the coaching profession. He became one of our sponsors and remains in the GCA as a member and is the Vice-President of the Board of Directors. Because of this connection, several of our members have had their articles published in choice Magazine.

Over the years there have been many signs of growth and development. In November 2019 one of our members, Arnie Katz, started our monthly newsletter and he's been very faithfully getting it out on a regular basis. He offers our members an opportunity to showcase their projects so all the members know what's going on.

We believe, along with many who've been in the coaching profession for twenty-five years, that the "Father" of coaching is Thomas Leonard, founder of Coach U and coachville.com. He is also a founder of the International Coaching Federation (ICF). I mention Thomas here to describe how much we appreciate him. To honor him, we set up an award that is given to one of our members who has shown a dedication to coaching and a path of service in coaching. It is called "The Thomas J. Leonard Humanitarian Award." This was first awarded in 2016 and has been given six times. In 2020, it was deferred and in 2021 we presented the award to two GCA members. (See Chapter 4 for more by Rick Reddington about Thomas, his life, work, and legacy. There is also more information about Thomas Leonard and the award on our website: www.thegaycoaches.com.)

In 2017, the leaders began to consider what would happen when we were no longer part of the alliance and we realized that we needed to incorporate so that we would have an entity to pass on the next generation. For a year or so, we worked with one of our leaders, Terry Hildebrandt, who coached us through the lengthy process of becoming a non-profit organization: filing all the forms, getting legal help, and forming a Board of Directors. It was a somewhat tedious process and, in the end, we ended up with most of the same men, only now we had titles and term limits. Normal turnover meant that some men left the board and they were replaced with a group of newer members. In May 2021, at the conference, several men left the board and newer members replaced them.

At the GCA Conference in May, 2019, we met a very energetic group of younger coaches who were very enthusiastic about the alliance and our mission. The leadership had the wisdom to create a new structure: conference planners who would be paid for their service. Since we had been a completely volunteer organization, this was a significant departure from our usual way of doing business.

Three men offered to take on this job: Chris Cooper, Shane Scott, and Peter Simmonds. It proved to be an inspired decision, as these men have proven to be gifted colleagues as well as impactful men. When our 2020 conference was cancelled because of Covid, they created our first virtual conference; when the future seemed grey, they created our first virtual winter conference; and they produced our 2021 Conference on April 30 – May 1, 2021.

At the first virtual Winter Conference, January 22 – 23, 2021, the membership in the GCA grew to exceed one hundred members. We believe that this growth can be attributed to the excellence of our virtual conferences as well as the regular postings on social media by our members, especially the younger ones.

Like the whole of society, the world seems to be changing rapidly and regularly. The GCA is experiencing these same changes and we remain devoted to our mission: to grow the number of gay coaches and to increase the number of gay men who are working with a coach. One of the meanings of the word "alliance" is to "further the common interests of its members." We remain committed to this purpose and, in doing so, we all hope to make a mark on the world and to leave a legacy of connection to the world, of influence on LGBTQ rights and justice, and of the power of a group to transform the culture.

4

WHEN PEOPLE ARE INSPIRED, THEY DON'T NEED MOTIVATION: COACHING AND THOMAS J. LEONARD

By Rick Reddington

Thomas J. Leonard (July 31, 1955 – February 11, 2003) was clear on the distinction between inspiration and motivation, and he was by far one of the most inspirational people I have ever met. Although his contribution and importance to the modern-day coaching industry is not widely recognized today, I would argue that Thomas was the Father of Coaching. Thomas was also a proud gay man, a recovering addict and alcoholic, an individual that occasionally grappled with depression and bi-polar disorder, as well as a brilliant entrepreneur and self-made business success story whose primary goal was to help others lead and live more authentically and completely.

Growing up in the San Francisco Bay area during the turbulent and transformative 1960s and 1970s, Thomas was influenced by these decades of cultural and societal change. Thomas always wanted to help people live better lives. Opting not to pursue a college degree, Thomas instead completed a series of correspondence courses that prepared him to become a Certified Financial Planner. Thomas then worked within the Accounting department of Werner Erhard and Associates (WEA) during the mid-1980s. WEA is best known for its controversial brand of human growth development and personal transformation workshops known as "est" and "the Forum." During this period, Thomas realized that many of his clients were hungry for more than just financial advice, they wanted life assistance, or what would eventually become known as life coaching.

In 1988, he left WEA and began to market and deliver his first course offering, the Life Planning Workshop. This content would evolve to essentially become the framework for the initial curriculum provided by CoachU, which Thomas founded in 1992. Always a popularizer and media machine even without today's sophisticated internet-based tools, Thomas grew CoachU aggressively, training over 7000 would-be coaches in thirty-eight countries within just a few years. Thomas led the growth and expansion of CoachU with his charisma, building a predominantly volunteer-based workforce which supported invaluable contributions at a low operational price point. It was a brilliant strategy. In 1994, Thomas also founded the International Coach Federation (ICF), primarily designed as an alumnus support function for CoachU. Thomas sold CoachU in 1996 for a handsome profit, allowing his entrepreneurial spirit to move forward creatively; it was never his intent to just manage any established business. Subsequently, he also separated from the ICF, as its purpose no longer aligned with his vision. Thomas, and the professional coaching industry, were ready to grow.

Throughout the next several years, Thomas became one of the foremost voices for advancing coaching. He was featured in over 200 international media outlets; authored five coach-related best sellers, including The Portable Coach; and collaborated on the creation of dozens of personal and professional development tools and programs, including A Perfect Life. He provided countless tips and techniques for how to grow and leverage any business, but particularly a coaching practice. He also recorded over a hundred hours of audio demonstrating various coaching techniques. At the same time, Thomas traveled the country in an RV with his dog Fringe, evangelizing the power and potential of coaching to anyone that would listen. Thomas believed that coaching could change the world, and that coaches could be the catalyst. In 1998, Thomas also launched Teleclass.com, a virtual collection of educational offerings delivered via conference-call technology, well before the online learning capabilities that exist today. Thomas was always ahead of his time.

I believe Thomas's most significant contribution was the creation of Coachville in 2000, the world's first and fastest-growing online coaching community. At the time, it was a one-of-a-kind information sharing, networking, connection, and learning experience. Thomas believed that the best way to dramatically expand the industry further was to provide unlimited access to countless coach training resources and tools. I was fortunate and grateful to be a Founding Member of Coachville. It was an exhilarating, empowering, and life-affirming experience. Of course, like many of his ideas, Coachville quickly grew and evolved, again leveraging the power and contribution of a predominantly volunteer-based development team. In response to member demand, the Graduate School of Coaching was launched by Coachville in 2001, delivering over 1000 hours of both live and recorded instructional content and coach training. One of the hallmarks of this era was the collaborative development of the Coachville Coaching System, a five-element methodological framework including the 15 Coach Proficiencies. Aspects of the behavioral attributes described within the proficiencies can still be found within every leading coaching model today.

Thomas was back on the road in early 2002, as Coachville hosted its first sold-out live conference in Las Vegas. The success of this event spawned a robust agenda of other more targeted workshops, and a full schedule of two-day Certified Coach Intensives, led by Thomas, around the USA and Canada. Coaches clamored to observe and learn from Thomas; it was an invigorating, transformative, experiential certification process. Thomas, Coachville, and the future of coaching were on a roll. In January 2003, Thomas co-founded the International Association of Coaches (IOC) as an alternative to the ICF. The IOC focus and coach certification process was significantly different from the ICF, and Thomas believed that the industry was ready for multiple pathways.

Amid yet another wave of growth and change for the coaching industry, Thomas passed away suddenly on February 11, 2003 from a massive heart attack. In the wake of his untimely death, other aspiring coaches and coach leaders stepped up to carry the work forward. Thomas's desire to see other people thrive and shine lived on in them.

Of course, Thomas was so much more than the accumulation of his accomplishments and contributions. Thomas championed everything about coaching because he genuinely believed that people could live better, more purposeful, and even happier, lives through coaching. He believed everyone could be a coach, but that those truly called to make a difference would lead the way. Thomas was an enigma: he flourished on the energy and excitement of others, yet preferred solitude. He was meticulously organized and fastidious, yet would often resist planning or scheduling until the last minute. He would instigate a big idea, but defer the development of details to others. Thomas had a larger-than-life persona and thrived in front of an audience, but was quite shy. He had a clever wit, a brilliant mind, a hearty laugh, a generous spirit, and a kind soul. Thomas could enroll others into his ideas without hesitation. He believed in the power of the group, although he was often clear on his own desired outcome. He could make you feel comfortable, valued, and safe. Thomas was a charismatic and transformational leader whose light still burns bright within many of us too.

THE COLLECTION

5

GAY MALE COACHES: IMPORTANCE OF SEXUAL IDENTITY DISCLOSURE AS PART OF BEING THEIR AUTHENTIC SELF

By David Whittleton

This writer's philosophy and approach to coaching executives is to "be of service to others and make an impact on their lives through his passion, genuineness and, most importantly, his authenticity." My client base runs the gamut of transgender individuals, gay men, and straight women because of my attitude toward sexual diversity and openness. Being authentic to one's true self is key to building a solid relationship, and being open about their sexual orientation adds value to the coach's own personal transformation journey.

While the relationship between working alliance and sexual orientation disclosure has received some attention in therapeutic literature, it has only just started being explored in coaching contexts. This chapter looks at understanding how your self-disclosure can strengthen relationships, instill trust, and boost your ability to inspire through the coaching experience.

Note: For the purpose of this discussion, the terms sexual orientation and sexual identity are used interchangeably.

Hiring a Professional Coach

It is no secret that successful people hire a coach to help them excel in their field and/or personal life. At times during coaching sessions, the client may feel raw and vulnerable as they confront the painful areas of their life and do the hard work of personal growth. The client's relationship with the coach, however, should be a safe place to cast aside their former life and greet the world with a new, more positive, better functioning perspective.

A strong coaching relationship is based on the building of an authentic relationship. Sharing similar backgrounds helps the client feel comfortable and safe to open up the conversation. It offers them a natural launch pad and ability to dive in right away. Clients want to know that the coach will "get" them—that they share a common understanding and do not have to "translate" to explain everything. For many, it increases the likelihood that they will establish trust and get to the heart of their work more quickly.

Connection is a key area in hiring a professional coach. The coach should be non-judgmental, yet willing to gently confront their client about ways they see them holding themselves back. The coach should be someone the client feels they can open up to, like a dear friend or partner with whom they can share personal details, and at the same time, be professional and maintain clear boundaries and confidentiality per International Coaching Federation (ICF) Core Competencies.[1]

The relationship and openness of the coach is going to be key in the building of trust between the coach and the client upfront in order to be successful throughout the course of the working relationship. Coaches choose to share certain biographical information with their clients to help build the coaching alliance. The coach who comes across as secretive about whether they have ever had children, are in a relationship with a partner, etc., is going to be trusted less. The challenge here is to maintain good professional boundaries while also being willing to relate to the client as an ally, an authentic human being, not an impersonal and distant professional.[2]

Kyle Elliott[3], a career coach in the San Francisco Bay Area, believes in building a relationship based on authenticity with his potential clients right from the very beginning. In an interview, Kyle stated that "the more I share about my lifestyle, the more people seem drawn to me" and being himself and fully open about who he is and his sexual orientation is part of who he is as a coach. He says that this level of authenticity on his part is appealing to all kinds of clients, and has attracted clients who are not gay, too.

Purposes of Self-Disclosure in Coaching

Coaching is all about authenticity, not masks. Consistent with this inclination is that the coach should self-disclose their sexual orientation as part of modeling behavior. By sharing more openly, coaches give their clients permission to do so as well. The coach comes across as less defensive and less guarded, and lets the client know it is okay for them to do so also. However, this is true of any coach/client relationship regardless of the sexual orientation of the coach and/or the client.

Self-disclosure also increases trust in the coaching relationship. It helps build the alliance by making the coach more real, more human. There is less of a top-down relationship and more of a side-by-side way of relating that communicates an intention that "we're working on this together." This helps balance the power in the relationship and empowers the client more.

As coaches self-disclose effectively it helps the client develop new perspectives. Seeing how someone else experienced a similar situation, but perhaps handled it differently, can open up some new possibility thinking. All of this can, at times, instill hope and encouragement.

The coach's self-disclosure can also help with the client's own self-acceptance as they realize "I'm not the only one." They may be reassured that their own reaction was not that unusual and that other people who have been through something similar have felt the same way.

Using self-disclosure in coaching can help open doors or close them (i.e., authenticity and transparency builds trust). The "coaching conversation" is different than a simple friend-to-friend chat. It's different than meeting folks at a party. The coaching conversation is a professional exchange of energy and ideas, of planning and possibility thinking. It is purposeful, conscious, and intentional, yet natural and entirely human. To be in this trusted space together and share for the purpose of growth and increased health and wellness means expressing who we truly are but doing so with a keen awareness of choice and responsibility.

The importance of self-disclosure by the coach was reinforced in a discussion with Jeff Nally[4], executive coach and president of Nally Group. He stated that "pulling back the curtain" with the client upfront and having the perspective of his background is key in establishing their relationship. When the coach is open about their life transformation by coming out and being out, it helps their client come out of their comfort zone and make the transformative changes they may be called to make in their life as a result of coaching.

Bernie Kettle[5] has a business and life coaching practice that primarily serves gay men who are on a personal/spiritual journey to be their authentic self (e.g., coming out). He brands himself as a "Mentor to Bold Ass Gay Men Everywhere" and his website includes images of gay men and other icons that support his mission of being a badass (i.e., fierce and powerful) gay man. Bernie focuses his practice on a specific subset of middle-aged gay men, which he himself is a part of, but is open to working with anyone who is looking for coaching. Because of this, Bernie believes his practice also benefits from the automatic preference that members of stigmatized groups have for fellow members.

How A Coach Responds Will Matter

Research shows that self-disclosure is most beneficial when it's a two-way process. People form the strongest bonds when they open up to one another in a way that they are both comfortable with.[6] However, you may be tempted to offer advice where it's not wanted. And you should resist the urge to tell your own story in response, even if you think it would show solidarity or understanding, as it risks trivializing or overshadowing the other person's news. Instead, give people the time and space they need to share their information. And respond sensitively, so that the value you place on their self-disclosure is clear.

Ryan et al. (2015)[7] points out that "sexual identity disclosure is a choice to express one's self authentically in the world." Deci and Ryan[8] argue that to the extent that this decision is accompanied by a sense of volition, it will be—by definition—an act of personal autonomy. It also ushers in bodies of (theoretical and empirical) knowledge that elucidate autonomy support factors in a variety of life domains and interpersonal contexts.

According to Ryan et al. (2017)[9], "autonomy-supportive responses" (defined as providing choice within specific rules and limits and acknowledging the other person's feelings and perspectives) are a robust predictor of being "out" as a gay, lesbian, or bisexual person.

Furthermore, an earlier study by Ryan et al.[10] revealed that how others react to disclosure can have a long-term impact on well-being.

Interestingly, their data indicated that an overt positive response was less important than an overt negative response (e.g., rejection). They concluded, "rather than requiring a carefully crafted, supportive, and politically correct reaction, disclosure may only need to be met with some measure of openness, or even just the absence of negativity from important others" (p. 564). They continued "autonomy-supportive responses can precisely provide this. Acknowledging personal perspectives and honoring choice do not demand grand displays of positivity. Rather they can be more subtly supportive, by simply thanking the person for sharing and recognizing their courage. When this is done, the experience should be free of negativity and (as recent research suggests) positively supportive of well-being."

When a client feels that the coach understands the "why" in their values, the coach establishes a trust that strengthens the relationship. Having trust in one another allows for more open communication and in return allows the coach to have a deeper connection with their clients.

A competent, trustworthy, and caring coach will be able to guide their clients to the best version of themselves. The stronger the coach/client relationship, the more honest and genuine conversation will be and, in turn, allow the client to achieve their desired results sooner and more efficiently.

Conclusion

Regardless of a coach's sexual identity, creating a coaching environment built on authenticity, where the client feels they are in a safe, confidential environment is what matters the most. When the coach demonstrates that they understand their client and respects their interests, values, and concerns, the client feels accepted. They can be honest about their thoughts and feelings and be more willing to try new behaviors. Sexual identity disclosure by the coach builds trust, enhances the overall relationship quality between stakeholders and leads to enhanced coaching outcomes.

Thus, I believe that a gay male coach using his own cultural and sexual orientation lens as a result of their own transformation experience is a better choice for clients and has an impact on the relationship between the coach and their client, regardless of their sexual orientation.

References

1. International Coaching Federation (ICF). (n.d.). Core Competencies. Retrieved 8 August 2021 from https://coachingfederation.org/core-competencies
2. Arloski, Michael 2012 Self-Disclosure in Coaching – When Sharing Helps and Hinders. https://realbalancewellness.wordpress.com/2012/03/02/self-disclosure-in-coaching-when-sharing-helps-and-hinders/, Accessed 8 August 2021.
3. Elliott, Kyle. Personal interview, 9 March, 2021.
4. Nally, Jeff. Personal interview, 3 March 2021.
5. Kettle, Bernie. Personal interview, 4 March 2021.
6. Susan Sprecher, Stanislav Treger, Joshua D. Wondra, Nicole Hilaire, Kevin Wallpe, Taking turns: Reciprocal self-disclosure promotes liking in initial interactions, Journal of Experimental Social Psychology, Volume 49, Issue 5, 2013, Pages 860-866, ISSN 0022-1031, https://doi.org/10.1016/j.jesp.2013.03.017.
7. Ryan, W. S., Legate, N., & Weinstein, N. (2015). Coming out as lesbian, gay or bisexual: The lasting impact of initial disclosure experiences. Self and Identity,14(5), 549–569.
8. Deci, E. L., & Ryan, R. M. (2000). The "what" and "why" of goal pursuits: Human needs and the self-determination of behaviour. Psychological Inquiry,11(4), 227–268.
9. Ryan, W. S., Legate, N., Weinstein, N., & Rahman, Q. (2017). Autonomy support fosters lesbian, gay, and bisexual identity disclosure and wellness, especially for those with internalized homophobia. Journal of Social Issues,73(2), 289–306.
10. Ryan, W. S., Legate, N., & Weinstein, N. (2015). Coming out as lesbian, gay or bisexual: The lasting impact of initial disclosure experiences. Self and Identity,14(5), 549–569.

6

WHAT A GAY COACH CAN OFFER STRAIGHT LEADERS

By Craig Howe

As a gay coach, I chose not to position myself as a coach exclusively to other LGBTQI+ individuals. Frustrated by many a poor leadership experience in my career in finance, I chose to try and improve this environment. I chose to bring my energy, passion, and care to bear on another group with significant challenges: leaders.

Six years on, I have had the honour and privilege to work with more than 500 leaders from over 45 countries around the world. I am not under any illusion that the battle for better leadership is won. While there have been some positive trends, more balanced representation at the board level has a long way to go. The measurement of success still tends to focus too narrowly on profit, rather than the positive impact an organisation can have on the societies in which they operate.

In this environment, I am intrigued by how my "gay" experience of the world supports me in working with so many straight leaders through my coaching. What equips me to achieve successful outcomes with such a diverse range of individuals?

By tapping into my experience of being in a minority group, I connect wholeheartedly with others. Theodore Roosevelt said, "Comparison is the thief of joy." I believe it. There tends to be an image or combination of attributes that we believe represents the ideal. Yet this is often an image that does not represent how most of us look, feel, or identify. Recognising how challenging being "other" can feel, I know compassion is essential.

In my role as coach, it is my responsibility to bring greater objectivity, revealing blind spots and perception gaps. The stereotypical leader tends to be directive, fast paced, and more interested in task than relationship. So many role models portray this style that it has become perceived as being the prerequisite for success as a senior leader. As such, many leaders feel pressured to conform to this image as they progress through the ranks during their career. They suppress their true nature and preferences, rather than risk standing out. The outcome of this can be entire leadership teams that are similar stylistically and at serious risk of group think.

I share honestly, challenge with kindness, and help the leader to map out a way forward. Leadership is demanding and can be overwhelming. In coaching, many leaders share information that they have never revealed before. Creating a safe space for the leader to slow down and be truly seen and heard without judgement, enables a shift deep within them. I also know that leaders can be somewhat isolated the more senior they become within their organisation. By dint of the power they hold over others, subordinates tend to withhold real challenges and instead say what they believe the leader wants to hear.

For me, most important of all is to encourage greater diversity in the truest sense of the word. That means diversity as it relates to identity, cognition, personality, and style. Every leader is unique in calling upon their particular rich diversity of knowledge, skill, and experience. Allowing this difference to shine out, rather than suppressing it, is key to creating a broader range of leadership role models. There is no one way, there is your way.

As there is no stigma attached to leadership, to "come out" may seem less relevant as a metaphor for leaders. Yet I believe this choice in what leaders reveal to whom and when is just as applicable. Each person must define their core values and/or behaviors. Through clarifying the anchors against which they will self-evaluate, leaders build accountability around their intentions. Choices become conscious; success measurable. By defining what their own version of leadership looks like, each leader then has only the small task of honouring it. There the real work begins.

7

GAY MALE COACHES AND NEW CLIENT BIAS: HOW "OUT" CAN WE BE?

By Brad Krueger

Introduction

As an owner of an independent business and executive coaching practice, I have speculated about the role gay sexual orientation plays in attracting new clients. Should we hide our sexual orientation all or some of the time? Or should we be completely open and even promote it? Ideally, we would like to be authentically open. Afterall, coaching requires a trusting relationship, and our sexual orientation might help potential clients get to know, like, and trust us faster than our competitors. At the same time, it would be naïve to completely ignore the possibility that being gay undermines the success of our business. This dilemma led me to explore the biases that influence client buying decisions and the experiences of professional coaches who identify as gay, queer, or homosexual and use he/him/his pronouns. Between November 2020 and January 2021, I anonymously surveyed twenty-eight professional coaches with this specific identity. Participant demographics included:

- Eighty-nine percent conduct business in the US, Canada, and the UK
- Ninety-one percent identify their gender ethnicity as "White"
- Seventy-five percent provide business, entrepreneurship, executive, or leadership coaching

It is important to recognise that a client's decision to hire a coach is influenced by seemingly insignificant features of social situations. Nobel Prize winning behavioral economists Daniel Kahneman[1] and Richard Thaler[2] have written extensively about the psychological basis of humans' economic choices. Specifically, much of their work clarifies the flawed automatic biases (i.e., preferences without conscious knowledge) that influences human behavior.

Knowing clients' economic decisions are influenced by automatic bias, I wanted to understand how they relate to sexual orientation. Harvard University's Project Implicit[3] has been assessing people's thoughts and feelings outside of conscious awareness and control since its founding in 1998. Its "Sexuality" assessment anonymously measures participants' association of gay, lesbian, and straight sexual orientations with their perception of good vs. bad and specific stereotypes. According to an April 2004 to December 2015 summary of their "Sexuality" assessment's data, forty-nine percent of their roughly 1.4 million participants had moderate or strong automatic bias for straight people.[4] Only ten percent had a moderate or strong automatic bias for gay people.

Interestingly, this bias is not limited to only straight people. Even some gay men have some degree of automatic bias for straight over gay people. According to Project Implicit, members of stigmatized groups (e.g., gay men) were found to have a moderate automatic bias for "more socially valued groups" (e.g., straight men) because of the negative connotations their cultural environment assigns to their stigmatized group.[5] Given that it was legal to fire gay people in twenty-seven states[6] until the Supreme Court ruled in 2020 that the Civil Rights Act prohibits discrimination based on sexual orientation, there is certainly precedent that straight people are more socially valued. A recent 2020 McKinsey and Company poll[7] also found that twenty-one percent of cisgender LGBQ+ people view their sexual orientation as the biggest personal barrier to getting a raise, promotion, or chance to get ahead. Only two percent of cisgender straight people have a similar concern.

A more in-depth analysis of Project Implicit's 2006-2013 data that was published by the University of California Press (Callabra) found that the automatic bias for straight people is declining.[8] However, the degree of decline was notably less among Black, Asian, male, conservative, and older groups. The largest declines in automatic bias for straight people were among Hispanic, White, female, liberal, and young adult participants and were notably larger for lesbian women than gay men.

Given that participants in Project Implicit's assessments are self-selecting, my hypothesis is that people taking their online Sexuality assessment are inherently curious about their personal bias and are not likely to be individuals who are overtly homophobic. This implies that their data is not a sample representative of the world's population and likely understates the true extent of automatic bias that exists for straight people over gay people. Even if automatic preferences for straight people have declined in recent years, I still believe it is safe to conclude that least half of the global population in developed countries still has a moderate to strong automatic bias for straight people.

The degree of bias is likely to vary up or down based on local environmental context (e.g., cities, rural areas, countries). All other personal attributes (e.g., gender, race, ethnicity, confidence level) being equal, simply being an openly gay male suggests one's overall pool of potential clients is significantly decreased as compared to a straight and even a lesbian coach. This data correlates with the experiences of surveyed gay male coaches, of whom only twenty-five percent believe that their sexual orientation has never deterred a potential client from hiring them.

Knowing there remains a significant automatic bias for straight people, gay male coaches are faced with the dilemma of how open they should be in their practice. In my survey, only sixty-one percent of coaches are open about their sexual orientation to most of their clients before they are hired and only forty-six percent publicize their sexual orientation. Many gay male coaches appear to recognize the existence of automatic bias for straight people and that being open about one's sexual orientation can artificially reduce their pool of potential clients. Since attracting coaching clients requires building a trusting relationship, gay coaches are further disadvantaged compared to straight peers if they cannot be their authentic selves.

Even though gay male coaches face headwinds presented by an automatic bias for straight people, some gay male coaches have decided to strategically publicize their sexual orientation as part of their approach to attracting clients. According to Project Implicit, members of stigmatized groups tend to have more positive automatic bias for fellow members of their group.[9] This automatic bias might explain why some clients might be more likely to pick a gay male coach over their straight counterpart. To better understand how these coaches are realizing success in the face of lingering bias for straight people, I interviewed two coaches who participated in the survey.

- Matthew Bennett has a global life and executive coaching practice that specializes in serving "LGBT+, kinky, and sex worker communities." He brands himself as the "English Leather Master" with explicit kinky online content. According to Matthew, he is the only explicitly kinky gay male coach in the world and eighty percent of his clients identify as gay men. His unique coaching persona appears to attract clients with similar identifies. While Matthew is successfully attracting the clients he does his best work for, he admits that his online erotic kinky persona potentially limits his career choices and client pool. For the safety of his family and to retain his professional network, he intentionally excludes the specifics of his coaching practice from his LinkedIn profile.
- Kyle Elliott has a career coaching practice that primarily serves tech workers who live in large metropolitan areas, including the San Francisco Bay Area, Austin, Texas, New York City, and Bengaluru, India. He brands himself as a career expert who helps clients get unstuck and own their fabulousness. Kyle publicizes his sexual orientation in subtle ways such as including the Gay Coaches Alliance logo on his website and posting pictures of him and his partner on social media. He has found that being authentic and vulnerable in his posts encourages more engagement and interest in his services. Unfortunately, it has also sparked overt bullying with some LinkedIn users posting homophobic slurs. Interestingly, Kyle's clients almost all identify as heterosexual men and women. As Kyle puts it, the people in the large cities he serves either don't mention his sexual orientation or go out of their way to mention how accepting they are of his sexual orientation. Being openly queer is just one way Kyle shows his authentic self to build trust with clients.

These individual stories illustrate the paradigm that gay male coaches face when openly including their sexual orientation as part of their business strategy. The prevailing automatic bias worldwide for straight people looms over all business relationships. Yet the strength of that bias varies greatly based on the local environment and who they serve. At times, there may even be an automatic bias for hiring them over a straight coach if they are a member of a unique stigmatized group of gay men that has an affinity for fellow members.

At this time, I believe gay male coaches still need to be strategic about publicizing their sexual orientation. There are examples of when incorporating one's sexual orientation into their business strategy positively differentiates a coaching practice from competitors. Likewise, there are plenty of examples where straight bias is alive and well and being too public could drastically shrink your potential client pool. Often it is hard to know why a potential client did not hire you. The decision whether to disclose sexual orientation may well be guided by the context and demographic of the clients you most want to work with.

Ultimately, I believe that being open about one's sexual orientation will be table stakes for building trust with potential clients. With the automatic bias for straight people slowly decreasing, I hope future coaches will not need to consider how open to be and one's sexual orientation will be no different than a person's eye or hair color.

References

1. Kahneman, Daniel. Thinking Fast and Slow. New York: Farrar, Straus and Giroux, 2011.
2. Thaler, Richard H., Sunstein, Cass R. Nudge. New York: Penguin Group, 2008.
3. Implicit Association Test (IAT) - Sexuality, https://implicit.harvard.edu/implicit/selectatest.html, Accessed 2/17/2020.
4. Project Implicit FAQs – Do gay participants show a preference for gay over straight? https://implicit.harvard.edu/implicit/faqs.html#faq10, Accessed 3/15/20.
5. Project Implicit FAQs
6. Freedom for all Americans, https://freedomforallamericans.org/states/, Accessed 2/28/2021
7. How the LGBTQ community fares in the workplace, McKinsey and Company, https://www.mckinsey.com/featured-insights/diversity-

and-inclusion/how-the-lgbtq-plus-community-fares-in-the-workplace

8. Westgate, E C et al 2015 Implicit Preferences for Straight People over Lesbian Women and Gay Men Weakened from 2006 to 2013. Collabra, 1(1): 1, pp. 1–10, DOI: http://dx.doi.org/10.1525/collabra.18
9. Implicit Association Test (IAT) - Sexuality.

8

THE WHY MATTERS

By John Carlson

After years of hard work, I finally had my dream job as a district manager for a major telecommunications company. At the age of twenty-four, I felt like I was on top of the world.

I knew I was hiding a big part of who I was, but I was used to it. I had been hiding this part of me for my entire life. I knew at the age of twelve that I was gay. Of course, I still had the playground marriage in third grade and the girlfriend throughout high school because that was "normal," right? I then saw that same "normal" play out in my adult life. I married my high school sweetheart. We were going to have kids and have a beautiful life because that was "normal."

I continued going through the motions, being "normal," and doing what was expected of me until a monumental event happened in my life. My father was diagnosed with brain cancer. We were given a prognosis of no more than eighteen months. A year and a half. The doctor said to my father, There are a couple options: fight aggressively, spend most of your time in hospitals, and eventually succumb to the cancer, or we perform one surgery that will give you the best quality of life while you are still here and you start deciding what to do with that time. My dad chose the latter.

What would you do if you had eighteen months to live? This question continued to resonate with me over the next few weeks and months. I was not living. I was hiding. I was playing house and playing make believe. I was a shell of my true self. While driving around one night I made the decision that I was done pretending. I was done hiding. Shortly after this decision, my wife and I filed for divorce, separated assets, and I moved out. I accepted a job with the telecommunications company I mentioned earlier, and I began actually living my life. I was going on dates with men and for the first time ever I knew what they meant by feeling fireworks exploding or seeing stars from a single kiss. I was living my authentic life.

With the acceptance of the new job came the decision of whether or not to be publicly out at work. I had no idea, in my own naiveté, that this decision would come with great ramifications. I decided that I was going to be unapologetically me, which meant being out at work. I placed a picture of my boyfriend in my cubicle and I was unafraid to talk about him with co-workers. During this time, a shift began to happen. Suddenly I was being told not to be too ya know? in front of clients: do not be one of those in-your-face gays, easy on the bent wrist, watch your inflection. These nuggets of wisdom were coming from leadership and from human resources, which should have told me all I needed to know. It was okay to BE gay but not to APPEAR gay.

I spent most of my life hiding that part of who I was. I was not going to continue that way of life. I had the unique opportunity to sit down with a member of the executive leadership team due to an award I won. I was able to share with her some of what I was experiencing and ideas I had to fix it. Two weeks later I received an email and a budget with the call to action of "let's make the workplace better for all." I was ignited. I found my calling. My career with DEI (Diversity, Equity, and Inclusion) work was born. I'm now a Talent Leader at livingHR. I facilitate workshops about how to create or transform DEIB (Belonging) programs, speak at panels on Diversity & Inclusion and culture, and host livingHR's "We Belong" podcast.

I am asked very often why I do what I do. My why is simple. We have all heard the business case for DEI work and its return on investment. However, at its core, DEI work is about people and creating cultures where the workforce means more than the transactional nature of their employment. They become meaningful assets to your organization in their individuality and full educational and lived experiences. So, it has become critical that organizations create environments where employees can bring their whole selves to it and feel that they truly belong. That is what I do. Martin Luther King Jr. believed in a land where all men, women, and children were viewed as equal. We ARE equal. It is time that we change the status quo and make his dream our reality and the reality for generations to come.

9

BEING A GAY COACH IN THE STRAIGHT CORPORATE WORLD

By Jeff Nally

My career in human resources, leadership development, and executive coaching has been in manufacturing and healthcare corporations in the midwestern U.S. Executive leadership teams were not diverse, headquarters were in rural areas, and there were no employee resource groups in those companies until the 2010s. I have been "out" since my late teens, progressed into senior leadership roles, and been a gay professional in HR and coaching for twenty-six years.

After I created the executive coaching practice and coached internally at a Fortune 100 company, a C-suite executive made an observation during a succession review that sparked my insights to the significance of being a gay coach in the straight corporate world. They said, "We've been successful growing our business, but we don't have enough leaders ready to keep growing or transforming this company. Leaders are copying our bad behaviors and they don't know who they are at their core or what their purpose is as a leader. This must stop."

My executive coaching practice became a hub of leadership transformation. My perspective and presence as a gay coach was pivotal to the transformation. I noticed key reasons I was sought out as gay coach in a straight corporate environment. Those reasons continued years later when I started my own coaching firm. Here's what I've learned from my work in the straight corporate world. I hope these ideas will help you to spark transformation in your coaching clients, too.

Gay coaches are living proof that transformation is possible. I led my transformation—twice! I transformed as I became aware of my sexual orientation and came out of the closet. And I transformed as I became a coach through my coach training experience, mentor coaching, coaching supervision, and coaching practice. Gay coaches intentionally explore and transform themselves, which can help our clients realize that intentional exploration and transformation are possible.

Gay coaches spark curiosity in straight leaders. I learned that straight corporate leaders feared their journey of self-awareness and transformation. Their identities were wrapped-up in career paths, job titles, and positions on the organization chart. But they didn't fear me. Instead, they were curious how my courage grew as a gay man in corporate leadership roles and how I rallied courage to become a coach. These experiences helped them grant me permission to guide them through reflection, self-awareness, stakeholder feedback, and the coaching process. When straight leaders want to know more about us as gay coaches, they shift from fear to curiosity to confidence in their own coaching experience.

Gay coaches accelerate trust with gay corporate leaders. Gay leaders hired me as their coach because I have first-hand experience with the same challenges they grapple with daily. The immediate credibility, familiarity, and shared experiences helped us accelerate coaching stages such as building trust, crafting coaching goals, and creating reflective practices.

Gay coaches are parents, too. Gay leaders who are considering parenting requested me as their coach because I pursued domestic and international adoption before it was legally recognized and have raised a son with my spouse. One gay leader in a high-tech firm prepared for a promotion while they were becoming a parent and mustering the courage to come out to the company. I coached another gay leader, newly hired as an executive in a Fortune 50 company, who struggled to create relationships with straight executives while attending to their spouse and children after relocating from an urban area to the Midwest. Our perspectives as gay coaches and parents help us connect with clients whose corporate roles impact their families.

Gay coaches help straight leaders "come out." My coming out experience helps me coach corporate leaders who are "coming out" to their own identities in life and work. After coaching a group of straight finance leaders to break down silos and "come out" to their conflicting relationships, one leader shared that they didn't want to be a finance professional any longer. Instead, they wanted to train finance leaders to be better people leaders. Their coming out disappointed peers and stifled promotion opportunities. They left the company and became a valued trainer and consultant to finance professionals in several organizations.

Gay coaches have survived exclusion and discrimination and thrived. Straight corporate leaders are more willing to share with me how they feel when they are excluded and judged as less-than what the organization expects from them. Straight leaders know their gay coach has survived and thrived despite exclusion and discrimination. I was the only person with whom many of my clients had ever shared their exclusion and discrimination experiences. Gay coaches are uniquely positioned to understand, empathize, and coach straight leaders on their journeys to greater inclusion and equality.

10

COMING OUT AND BEING OUT IN THE WORLD: HOW INSIGHTS FROM THE COMING OUT PROCESS SUPPORTS A COACHING MINDSET

By Tony V. Zampella

As gay coaches, we can access our shared experience of "coming out" to serve our clients if we use it as a model for becoming whole. The process of coming out involves a cycle of asking, acting, and accepting.

- We ask questions from a different viewpoint. Rather than "What is wrong with me? Why am I not normal?" which results in diagnoses and seals us in our closets, we ask, "What is happening? What am I observing or experiencing?" to open possibility.
- We act on our discoveries courageously. Action expands awareness of our role in participating in the creation and definition of our relationship with the world outside.
- We accept our individual uniqueness as "different" (unique), rather than developing competence in performing "normal." This agency invites integration and inquiry, evolving consciousness with each cycle.

Exercising this generative capacity—"coming out" as asking, acting, and accepting—cultivates possibility, aliveness, and renewal. It is the antidote to our closet as gay men. Universally, this capacity also expands humanity, where fear and denial closet us by making us conceal and withhold our unique selves.

Insights from the coming out process support a coaching mindset. Rather than examining concepts in a "normative, problem-solving method" to "fix behavior," coaching embraces an "ontological approach" via inquiry into our emotions, bodily sensations, and language to "experience the nature of being."

As gay men, we may take for granted the fundamental lessons, skills and practices revealed by the coming out process. Since we do not have visible markers such as skin color or sexual organs that identify us as gay, we are what we say about ourselves. We affirm our dignity in the face of society's hostility. Our unique experience of inquiry and integration supports our work as coaches to serve others in their pursuit of becoming whole.

This chapter examines four interdependent structures and practices that constitute being human. Each is related to "coming out" inside a coaching model for becoming whole. "Self-awareness" cultivates our observer, clarifying self-perception; "integrity" strengthens our word, developing workability; "authenticity" opens possibility, discovering self-expression; and "commitment" prioritizes care, expanding dignity.

1. Self-Awareness As Observer

Human beings can be said "to be" because of our ability to see, perceive, feel, and interpret. Our self-awareness cultivates the "observers" we are as "being" human. We become attentive to the effects of the filters, maps, and blind spots in our interactions. Our observer reflects on discoveries and interprets what the world discloses.

Self-awareness reveals the nature of being as projecting views and then seeking evidence to confirm them. "What you don't know you don't know" is home to many of the blind spots that limit our perceptions, listening and perspectives.[1]

Seeing reality begins with continually stripping away our self-deceptions and dissolving any delusions. Consider the inner observer that led to your coming out. Recall when this stripping away of beliefs and delusions encouraged questioning and self-discovery to embrace your queer identity. Becoming whole begins with self-awareness.

Inquiry. To further develop our observer, cultivate our self-perception and sort out projections, we surround ourselves with different perspectives and invite or welcome feedback. Multiple perspectives and discoveries require the adoption of humility to seek questions rather than know solutions.[2]

Practices. Coaching supports practices such as pausing to clarify perceptions that precede behavior or performance. We pause between events (communications, meetings, situations, or activities) and before speaking to support mindfulness. In Sanskrit, mindfulness means "to remember." We pause to remember what we care about, and our current frame of reference, such as our roles, functions, jobs, or agreements.

2. Integrity As Word

Integrity is accountability to our word for the purpose of creating "workability" in our life. The process of coming out is a profound example of the power of our word to create workability. Recall the intense unworkability of living in the closet.

To constitute ourselves as our word requires "transparency about what one is giving one's word to, to whom it is being given, and by when the promise given by the word will be executed."[3]

Such an inquiry requires self-awareness to examine and discover when we are "in" or "out" of integrity—whether I can be counted on to act as I have stated. Unfortunately, socialization views integrity through morality (being virtuous), through ethics (the right standards) or as normative (ideal behavior). In this context, examining our word often occurs as an assault on our moral or ethical character rather than an inquiry into the missing conditions necessary to restore our word.

Coaching observes integrity as "the state of being whole and complete." This descriptive view of integrity is important to individuals, groups, organizations and society because collective action requires workability for coordinating with and "counting on each other's word: a word kept by making and fulfilling commitments. If people let each other down, performance suffers, trust disappears, and anxiety reigns…"[4]

Optimal workability supports how we participate in co-creating our communities and belonging in them; the effective coordination and collaboration in everyday agreements, structures, and practices; and the cultivation of our dignity. All we can ever be is who we say we are.

Inquiry. Coaching examines the "unworkable" areas of life that undermine our effective coordination. Common areas of "out-integrity" include stepping over items that go against values, agreements, or self-respect; inaction, when we could have acted but didn't; and not acknowledging broken agreements.

Practice. Coaching supports by bringing "intention" to our word, pausing before creating agreements, clarifying promises and requests, completing any incomplete items, and creating more space in your schedule to become mindful.

3. Authenticity As Possibility

Authenticity exists between one's actuality, the "everydayness" of our world and one's possibility. Participation in the world finds us swept up by norms and conforming to "fit in." Through expanding responsibility for our "own-most possibility," we extricate ourselves from society's "expectations" to accept individual freedom.

That first momentous experience of coming out marks a unique experience when gay men reject society's expectations. The anxiety and anticipation preceding that moment blind us to a future possibility.

By exploring being, we integrate the whole self (mind, body, and language) and its origins (culture, identities, and heritage) to take custody of its narrative. With agency and autonomy, we hold ourselves accountable for living up to our possibility. We become responsible for who we are, who we've been and who we're becoming. We risk norms and others' expectations to realize our uniqueness rather than conceal or deny who we are. We become fully self-expressed.

Being gay is more than machinery in bed. Accepting our identity involves owning what it means to be gay in the world. To own liberation in 2021 is to appreciate "gay existence" in nineteenth-century Paris, 1945 Germany or 1969 New York City. Beyond trivial facts, these psycho-socio-political-historical aspects constitute our selfhood, community, and culture. Authenticity strengthens the process of integration, a necessary state for becoming whole.

GRID A: COMING OUT STRUCTURES © 2021 Tony Zampelia for Bhavana Learning Group www.bhavanalearning.com

CAPACITY/ STRUCTURE	DESCRIPTION	LINK TO "COMING OUT"	COACHING STRUCTURE	PRACTICES
Self-Awareness (To observe and discover)	Become attentive to filters, maps and blind spots in our interactions.	Increased awareness invites us to strip away delusions and enable self-discovery to reveal projections and truths.	**Observer.** Discern projections and view reality as what is from what it ought to be.	Pausing and mindfulness to check-in, feel and remember what we care about.
Integrity (To create workability)	The state of being whole and complete as in-tended (designed).	Experience the power of our word to declare "self" and create workability.	**Word.** Strengthen our word to create workability and co-create our world.	Examine areas of unworkability to align agreements, values, practices and structures.
Authenticity (To cultivate possibility)	Accountable to live our possibility as responsible for who we are, who we've been, and who we're becoming.	Experience liberating the self from normative ideals to the possibility of becoming whole and integrated.	**Possibility.** Own our uniqueness and potentiality — for the sake of our end.	Examine the pretens-es and expectations that undermine our possibility. Become self-expressed.
Commitment (To resolve what matters most)	Standing for something (a future) bigger than oneself.	The experience of taking a stand invites us to declare an authentic future.	**Care.** The "matter-ing structure" that connects being with its world.	What matters lives in language; reframe situations to gener-ate commitments.

View this grid as a interdependent whole with columns and rows as part of a system of thought and meaning.

Inquiry. Whether gay or non-gay, coaching supports self-discovery, truthfulness, and the integration of our experiences (mind, body, and language) with our culture, identities, and heritage to bring meaning to our existence. Through skillful listening, observing, and questioning, coaching unpacks pretenses via inquiry into inconsistencies, defenses, avoidance, or denial; it is designed to accommodate expectations that ignore our needs or undermine our possibilities.

Practice. Self-discovery resulting from candid reflection—a level of openness, accuracy, and awareness to communicate truth-telling reveals underlying needs that preserve pretenses.[5] Coaching dissolves the constraints on self-expression that support our embrace of our uniqueness. Moreover, self-discovery emerges for both the client and the coach, acknowledging shared qualities through reflective dialogue that reveals the commitments we are for others.

4. Commitment As Care

The word "commitment" can elicit confusion or angst. Whether bills, education, relationships or work, our lives depend on creating agreements that require commitment. Viewing commitment as a context for living involves standing for something bigger than oneself, such that our commitment becomes who we are.[6]

Reaching beyond one's self evokes our primal connection to others, which stems from learning how to be human from others. That initial "care structure" constitutes "mattering," giving meaning to our existence. What matters most lives through commitment to a set of concerns.

Self-fulfillment comes not from a focus on one's self per se. Instead, we are "concernfully absorbed by that … which meaningfully weave[s] our lives...".[7]

Commitments cannot be compulsive, like attachments that cause obsessions, nor commanded, like obligations that cause compliance. Authentic commitment emerges freely in an uncertain future. It necessitates "care" as a structure for being resolute in the face of changes, trade-offs and setbacks that invariably emerge, and requires taking a stand in the face of "the lostness in possibilities" that can provoke guilt.[8]

Simultaneously, the uncertain future that commitments evoke enliven and call forth possibilities while revealing greater doubt, disbelief, and insecurity.[9,10] Coaching normalizes this paradox to reframe experiences and (re)discover priorities.

For gay men, the prospect of coming out necessitates care for truth and commitment to change in the face of an uncertain world. Taking that stand alters how every aspect of our world occurs to us. We continue to frame this commitment with each expression of our identity beyond our initial coming out.

Inquiry and Practice. An authentic commitment is neither given nor purchased. We embody it in language by framing events and choosing paths. We summon all previous structures and practices—self-awareness, pausing, mindfulness, workability of word, authentic choosing and owning possibility—to generate a commitment that cultivates aliveness.

Summary

These four interdependent capacities serve as structures to access lessons from our shared coming out experience for the purpose of becoming more whole. As a way of being, this requires a commitment that demands the awareness of self-discovery, the integrity to act with dignity and the authenticity to account for our possibility.

As coaching professionals, the "coming out experience" offers unique access to the human condition, which we can use to serve our clients.

References

1. Souba, W. A New Model of Leadership Performance in Health Care. Academic Medicine, 86(10), 2011.
2. Kofman, F. Conscious Business: How to Build Values Through Values. Boulder Colorado: Sounds True, 2006.
3. Souba, W. The Being of Leadership. Philosophy, Ethics, and Humanities in Medicine, 6(1), 5, from http://www.peh-med.com/content/6/1/5, 2011.
4. Souba, W. A New Model of Leadership Performance in Health Care…
5. Dethmer, J., Chapman, D., & Klemp, K. The 15 Commitments of Conscious Leadership: A New Paradigm for Sustainable Success. Self-published, 2015.
6. Souba, W. A New Model of Leadership Performance in Health Care…
7. Anton, C. Selfhood and Authenticity. Albany: SUNY Press, 2001.
8. Zimmerman, M. Eclipse of the Self: The Development of Heidegger's Concept of Authenticity. Ohio: Ohio University Press Books, 1986.
9. Kofman, F., & Senge, P. Communities of Commitment: The Heart of Learning Organizations. Learning Organizations: Developing Cultures for Tomorrow's Workplace (Chawla, S. & Renesch, J., Eds.), pp. 14-43. Portland, Oregon: Productivity Press, 1995.
10. Senge, P. The Fifth Discipline: The Art & Practice of The Learning Organization. New York: Doubleday, 1990.

11

RESETTING MY EXPECTATIONS

By Thomas M. Keydel

In my work with clients, I'm asked to offer myself to their challenges and to more fully understand and appreciate where they are now and who they are choosing to be as they move forward. Yes, every client is naturally creative, resourceful, and whole and every client is completely unique. Yet, broadly speaking, there are similarities of heart, mind, and spirit which make my clients accessible and understandable to me. I'm listening for that. The qualities of endurance, focus, and grit count for a lot. I also try to remember that not everything works out exactly as expected. Commitments run their natural course. The relationships that we have with our goals are, themselves, living things. So, as I work with my clients, I am reminded of a simple fact: no one is a "blank slate." We are where we are because of everything that brought us to our present moment.

I know how difficult it can be to remember that. Unconsciously, we might see ourselves in our client's choices and decisions; potentially, we might hold an artificial hope for our client's choices and decisions because, at one time, that same goal was important to each of us. How, we might ask, do our expectations coordinate with our deepest needs and does that bring forward our best self? Coaches have their own work to do. As much as we try to put that aside in favor of our client's work, it takes a great deal of patience and self-awareness. To grow because we choose to help others burdens us with a kind of distance that reorients many of our aspirations. Here is a story that illustrates the challenge we face and also why the work we do can be so fulfilling.

The Day My Balloon Disappeared

I took a breath and then I blew out my deepest desire into a balloon: "An eternity of compassion-based self-expression."

I took another breath and blew out the same desire over and over until the balloon was tight, round, and taut. Then, I tied it onto a string and carried it with me wherever I went—never letting it out of my sight.

Until one day a great blast of wind came off a mountain top and my balloon was snatched away from me.

Now, I suppose that was inevitable. Our deepest desires always have a way of slipping away from us. We do seem to lose sight of them, no matter how hard we might try.

Life's primordial conflict—between our dependence on our deepest wish and the reality that denies that wish—can create a lot of pain. It never seems to make any sense. How can a balloon be so dependent on the air around it when the balloon itself is so full of air? Don't they share a common reality?

I pondered that for a long time.

Without my balloon to remind me and to re-commitment it, my desires seemed to change in unexpected ways. "An eternity of compassion-based self-expression." That wasn't exactly right anymore. I had other newer commitments and interests.

Then I understood. "Eternity" meant my being true to myself. "Compassion" meant my standing with and for someone else. "Self-expression" meant the hard work letting go of any conflict between my reality and my dependence on my commitments and interests.

Later, I walked along the sandy beach and, surprisingly, my lost balloon appeared in front of me.

It was being pushed onto shore by the waves.

It looked so small. Deflated and abused. My former balloon was covered with dirt and with black algae and when it touched the shore, the wind pushed it past my feet and up onto the dunes and over the sea grass on top of it.

The air inside and the air outside are very much the same—and still—we are persuaded to see them as opposites.

The dream we hold inside our hopes—that doesn't disappear; however, it might get knocked about and changed, in unexpected and perhaps, even tragic ways.

It isn't possible for me to do this work, to be the best coach I can be, without resetting my expectations. To know that today is different from yesterday and how tomorrow will be different yet again. The surprising thing is how fulfilling that kind of freedom can be. Yes, I can choose to be present right now without making today a reflection of my former self and without equating any difference in my expression as some tragic disappointment. A potential adjustment—oh yeah, for sure. But every path moves on its own breath of interest and commitment, which itself must be a trusted place of repair and rest, before we can be led in a new direction. In the end, we only have ourselves with whom to make peace.

12

COACHING THE SUPERHERO: STANDING IN YOUR CLIENT'S GREATNESS

By Jerry Kajpust and Brian Gorman

Superhero Coaching

It is our practice to rarely take notes while coaching. We want our clients to capture their own insights. We encourage them to take notes by hand; this helps the brain retain the information better than capturing them on a keyboard. We allow clients to record our sessions if that works better for them; recording allows them to observe themselves, re-listen to questions, and hear their answers. One of the few sets of notes we do take is when doing superhero coaching.

What is superhero coaching?

Superhero coaching is just what it sounds like. It is coaching to identify a client's superheroes and put them to work on the client's behalf. Our superheroes embody the mindsets and behaviors we want for ourselves. Sometimes they are characteristics of ourselves that are already strong and well-developed. Other times they may be alien to us, but something we aspire to.

Why superheroes?

One of the questions we are taught to ask as coaches is, "Who do you have to be in order to...?" This can be a difficult question for clients to answer. Most of us don't spend much time thinking about our own being. Our superheroes represent who we want to be or who we have to be to face and move through our difficult challenges.

How are superheroes identified?

Step 1: Ask questions. For some people it can be "Who are your superheroes?" The answers pour out. A client's superheroes may be real, fictional, or a blend. They may include famous people as well as people you've never heard of. When coaching superheroes, always invite clients to really dig deep. "Who else?" "Who else?" "Who else?"

We know that some clients will be totally thrown off by the "Who are your superheroes" question. It doesn't mean that they don't have them; it's only that they don't think in those terms. This is often the case with the executives we work with. For them, shift the language, but not the intent. "Who do you look up to in business?" or "Who are your role models?" may be where to start. While superheroes typically span the personal and professional, role models often don't. When one of these two questions comes first, the next question we ask is, "Who do you look up to (or who are your role models) outside of work?"

Step 2: Once you have a full inventory of the client's superheroes, walk through the list to find out why each person is on the list. "What about Mother Teresa makes her a superhero for you?"[1] "Why is Harvey Milk on your list of superheroes?"[2] Now your client is describing his own "being" aspirations. Of all the things he may call out about each one, he is selecting the few characteristics that are important to him. As his coach, this is essential information going forward.

How do you put superheroes to work?

Anytime you want your client to focus on the "being" needed to take on a challenge, you can put his superheroes to work. Begin by listening to your intuition. Do you have a strong sense of the superhero the client would call on? If so, you might ask, "What would Mother Theresa do in this situation?" Or "How would Harvey Milk suggest you address this?" Alternatively, you might ask which superheroes your client can count on for assistance in facing the challenge he identified. Then move into how the named superhero(es) can assist and use the client's insights to guide him in the development of his action plan.

Coaching superheroes in action: Case 1 – "Arthur"

Arthur first began coaching with one of the authors when he was a high school junior. He had set his vision on attaining a Nursing PhD and then creating a blended career of nursing, teaching, and applied academic research. He was a pole vaulter on his school's track team. As a gay student interested in nursing, Arthur had a small social network and was not finding his academic curriculum as challenging as he wanted it to be. Whenever he asked his teachers to help him learn more, the reply was, "Study harder so you get better grades." Arthur lived with his mother who was very supportive of his career plans and hired a coach to help him navigate his way into college.

His coach wrote the following information about Arthur's superheroes.

Helen Keller[3]	Committed to learning even when she was not supported by those around her
Patricia (his mother)	Loves unconditionally
Harvey Milk	Out. Proud. Fought for what he believed in despite any odds
Terry Fox[4]	Invincible spirit. Found ways to pursue his goals even when the odds were against him (Terry Fox was a Canadian athlete who lost a leg to cancer. In 1980, with a prosthetic limb, he began a run across Canada to raise money for cancer research. His cancer forced him to quit his run, and eventually cost him his life; by the time he stopped, Terry had run over 3,300 miles in 143 days. The annual Terry Fox run now takes place in over 60 countries, raising money for cancer research.)

The first challenge Arthur took on with his coach was his desire to learn more, not study more.

Coach: "In a way this sounds like the challenge your superhero Helen Keller faced; in fact, some believed that as a deaf, blind, and mute young girl she couldn't learn at all. Yet she did. How might Helen Keller guide you to learning more?"

Arthur looked into the distance. His brow furrowed. Then he smiled. "She would tell me to find teachers who were willing to see the importance of learning to me and who would be open to guiding me in that learning. They might be in my school, but they might not be. They're non-traditional teachers, maybe in the nursing profession or researchers, people in the fields that I am interested in who are willing to nurture the interest and growth of someone motivated to learn from them." By the end of the coaching session, Arthur had identified three individuals who might serve in this teaching role for him and had developed a plan for approaching them.

His senior year, Arthur developed a significant hip problem that was going to require surgery. It became so bad that he had to use crutches and was then confined to a wheelchair. Not only did he have to sit out much of his final season on the track team, but Arthur was also finding it difficult to get around school and to focus on his studies. It was time for his coach to call on Arthur's superheroes again.

Coach: "Arthur, in our work together you identified several superheroes. Who can you call on to help you find your path forward now?"

This time, Arthur hardly hesitated. He almost shouted his answer. "Terry Fox and Harvey Milk!"

Coach: "Why those two?"

Arthur explained that they both took on challenges bigger than themselves: Harvey as a leader in the fight for gay rights in San Francisco in the early 1980s and Terry running to raise money for cancer research after losing his leg to the disease. Arthur observed that each had built a coalition of supporters to help them work toward achieving their goals. "I need to stop trying to do this on my own," Arthur said. "It's time to build my team!" Working with his coach, Arthur identified individuals in his circle of friends and members of the track team who could help him navigate getting to and from school and moving from class to class.

Then his coach asked, "Who do you need on your team to help you keep focused on your schoolwork?"

Not surprisingly, Arthur wanted the energy and spirit of both Harvey Milk and Terry Fox. Then he named his mother.

"What will she bring to the team?" Arthur's coach asked.

"She loves me unconditionally. She sees me hurting physically and emotionally and is willing to let me slack off. But if I ask her, she will also hold me accountable for staying focused, and I need that now." Working with his coach, Arthur formed a plan for building his team, including printing out pictures of Harvey Milk and Terry Fox to tape to the arms of his wheelchair.

Coaching superheroes in action: Case 2 – "Will"

Will was a mid-career professional when he began working with a coach. While successful, he was also dissatisfied with how he showed up. Like many gay men of his generation, he grew up "in the closet." He still tended to be quiet in the company of others, careful about whether to voice an opinion and, if so, how to say what was on his mind without offending anyone. What he saw as being of service to others many saw as being servile. In a recent performance review, Will's supervisor told him that sometimes it seemed that Will was working for those who reported to him rather than the other way around.

One of the authors often invites clients to create their future story. In doing so, they are encouraged to write the story from the future, not about the future; stories about the future tend to be head-centered while stories from the future are more often head, heart, and gut-centered. Here is part of the story Will wrote.

"The person I am is the hero of my own story—the person people are drawn to but, more importantly, the person who I am drawn to be. The person who has good days and bad days but at the core is peaceful and passionately himself. Who is open, honest, and on a spiritual path. I am the person who loves himself more than others so I can love others more.

"As my superhero I possess the following powers:

- I focus on one thing at a time.
- I am present in the here and now.
- I am not overwhelmed.
- I am being the best version of me.
- I am a spiritual being."

"I walk into a room and people feel these qualities. I feel these qualities. These qualities also repel any shame that may arise within me. I am wearing a superhero cape and these five qualities make up the colors of the cape. I display these qualities whether I am in the boardroom or at home with my family. I have this peace and charisma that is hard to describe."

Will has now set his goal on becoming his superhero. His coach is guiding him on the journey.

In Summary

The superheroes and the characteristics our clients call out represent the people they hope to become. Superhero coaching can be a powerful way to help them achieve their aspirations.

References

1. Mother Theresa – Biographical – Nobel Prize, https://www.nobelprize.org/prizes/peace/1979/teresa/biographical/
2. The Official Harvey Milk Biography, The Harvey Milk Foundation: https://milkfoundation.org
3. Helen Keller: Deaf, Blind Author and Activist Mini-Biography: https://www.youtube.com/watch?v=oxiJ02-hpZY
4. The Terry Fox Foundation: https://terryfox.org

13

WORKING THROUGH SELF CRITICISM TO REACH SELF LOVE

By Cator Sparks

Disabled

How often do you make a small mistake and your self-criticism just explodes? *You are so stupid. How could you do this again? My partner must think I am a f*#&ing idiot.* This happened to me a few weeks ago when booking an appointment online. I screwed it up twice and the person had to email me and remind me how to do it. I felt stupid, like I used to in school.

When I was very young, my mom started taking me to see therapists concerning my slow learning. I remember doing building blocks in an orange room with a big mirror on one wall. I knew there was someone watching me through the glass and it made me nervous and insecure. Around second grade I was diagnosed with a "Learning Disability."

That's all I knew. I think that is all my parents knew. It was shortened to "LD" on papers I would fill out. At seven years old, I was "disabled." That's all I heard. Stack that on top of being effeminate and bullied—life sucked. Mom and Dad didn't know. I put on the happy face around them and family members. I also had about eight pets to care for and they brought me tremendous joy. They needed me. They didn't care that there was something "wrong" with me.

Visionary Spirit

When I unloaded all of this on my coach he said, "I am mad at those people for labeling you with that term 'Learning Disability.' Why couldn't they say he is a Visionary Spirit?" Those words pierced my heart and the floodgate of tears came pouring out. I cried for days just thinking about the "what if" and for the fact that I felt so understood.

To get where I wanted to go, I developed a strategy on how to survive. I need to work extra hard not to fail. I exceeded in that through my personality, style, writing, and social life. I have lived a life I never dreamed existed. But that wounded part of my ego still is hungry and angry and scared. It feeds off of those perceptions that I am still not "enough." It's suspicious at best and vicious at worst. I wanted to numb the pain of feeling inadequate. Years of drinking till I blacked out or dipping into a bag of blow to feel funnier, more lovable, more validated. Until it all wore off. That version of ego will find anything to remind you of your inadequacy, which is a total lie. We call it a Core Lie: the core lie is that you are less than.

What I have learned is that I have spent so much time proving something that was already there. I am amazing just the way I am. Nothing needed to change. I simply had to relax and evolve and flourish. We spend too much effort proving something that doesn't actually require any proof.

Twice Exceptional

Friends of mine who have children who are very bright but learn differently are often referred to as "twice exceptional." They learn to talk about how they learn best, build strategies, and then advocate for themselves. How empowering! Self-love is vital for those of us who don't feel validated by society (pretty much all of us). Here are a few tips to keep handy when you knock that glass over, have a fender bender, or realize you have TP stuck to your shoe at that cocktail party:

Forgiveness: Calling ourselves "stupid" and "dumb" does nothing but make us feel worse. When you feel those words coming up, stop, and re-wire to remind yourself that you are enough. Practice forgiveness and, honey, LET IT GO.

Surrender Control: For me, when I screw up an appointment or get something wrong, I feel out of control. Surrender that too! I have actually started to take risks like raising my hand three or four times in each coaching class. If I get it wrong, so what? I tried.

Gratitude: This is one practice I encourage all of my clients to do. We can get bogged down in the "what I didn't do today" scenario.

Write five things you are thankful for every evening. It could be crossing everything off your list or just staring at your cat for an hour, which brought you joy. Congrats, you did it!

Laugh/Smile: If your day is sucking, call a friend, pick a flower, turn on some Diana Ross.

Talk it Out: I would have never released this trauma without talking it out. Let's head to baggage claim and rip those old trunks open and Marie Kondo your past. If it's not bringing you joy, let it go.

14

DELIVERING HARD TRUTHS: CRAFTING FEEDBACK WITHOUT TRIGGERING TRAUMA FOR GAY COACHES OR THEIR CLIENTS

By Jeff Nally

Gay coaches and gay clients have experienced the emotional scars of unsolicited feedback about who they are as humans. Bullies verbally or physically abused gays, and family members shared their disapproval of a gay person's identity and sexual orientation. Messages from the media, religious leaders, and institutionalized discrimination generated "feedback" that gays are less than other humans, excluded, and demeaned.

Since feedback in coaching can trigger defensive responses in our brains, there are practical applications for gay coaches to gather stakeholder feedback, review feedback with clients, and share hard truths.[1] There's neuroscience, next practices, and feedback research to guide gay coaches and help gay or straight clients receive feedback and move forward.[2]

Why We Hate Feedback

It's not our fault. It's our brain's fault. The phrase "I need to give you some feedback," triggers areas of the brain that create a threat response. Understanding how these areas of the brain work together, gay coaches can dampen the threat response during the feedback process for clients and teach them to do the same.

- Feedback triggers an emotional response in the amygdala, part of the limbic system. The emotional response is primary and impacts the coach's and client's subsequent thoughts and responses.

- The emotional response can prompt past experiences and memories from long-term memory where gay coaches and gay clients recall the trauma of bullying, the failure of workplace feedback systems, or the fear of other people's opinions of gay human beings.

- When delivering hard truths or unexpected feedback, the goal is to dampen the emotional threat response and quiet past experiences and assumptions so the client can learn from useful, meaningful feedback. Receiving feedback begins in the prefrontal cortex where the brain pays attention to feedback, ponders it, and remains curious about its meaning and usefulness. It's where insights spark motivation to act or change behaviors, and that's a valuable purpose of feedback.[3]

The following guidance helps brains to dampen the emotional threat of feedback, quiet negative experiences with feedback, and open the prefrontal cortex to be curious about the meaning and usefulness of feedback in the coaching experience.

Co-Create the Feedback Experience

Generate Certainty, Clarity, and Safety

For gay clients especially, certainty, clarity, and safety are essential to ensure the feedback process doesn't unintentionally trigger past trauma or unnecessary stress. This can be particularly threatening in workplace coaching where 360-degree feedback is used to gather perspectives and input on the client's coaching goals from a variety of participants including direct reports, peers, managers, senior executives, or other influencers on the gay client's career path.[4]

Coaching settings outside the workplace, like life coaching engagements, can also trigger past trauma as feedback participants may include family, friends, spouses, children, and others who influence the future relationship with the gay client. The stakes are high when stakeholders might provide painful feedback about a client's identity, values, beliefs, or sexual orientation.

To mitigate stress, the coach co-creating the feedback experience with the client can provide:

- Certainty about how the feedback will be gathered and shared

back to the client.
- Clarity in the context of why feedback is useful and how it is meaningful to the client's coaching goals.
- Safety for the client and feedback participants by explaining how confidentiality and/or anonymity will be maintained.[5]

Co-Craft the Feedback Items

Focus feedback on the client's coaching goals. If established or standard feedback surveys are used, share the context of coaching with the client and feedback participants. Interview-based feedback offers flexibility to co-create feedback items.
- Ask the client to craft ten feedback questions.
- As the coach, craft ten feedback questions.
- Share, compare, and contrast the questions.
- Review and refine until the client feels confident in the questions.

Dampen the gay client's threat response by focusing on the participant's perspective and direct experience, not generalized opinions or personal attacks on identity or sexual orientation. For stakeholder feedback, consider asking:

- What can the client stop doing to achieve the coaching goals?
- What can the client start doing?
- What can the client continue doing?
- What's the biggest opportunity for improvement?
- What's the biggest challenge?
- What emotions do you experience interacting with the client?
- What emotions would you experience if your relationship were even better?
- What do you want/need from the client?
- What will you experience when the client achieves their coaching goals?
- What can the client do to better support you?
- What words describe your relationship?
- What word describes your relationship when their coaching goals are achieved?
- What's the one question we didn't ask that will help the client?

Put the Client in Control of Launching the Feedback Process

Gay clients who experienced bullying or discrimination have received unsolicited "feedback" and judgment that can spark fear of proactively asking for feedback from people who are close to them. Another way to dampen that threat response is to put the client in control of launching the feedback process.

- Ask the client to create the initial list of feedback participants.
- As the coach, ensure key stakeholders are included.
- Ask the client whose voices and perspectives are missing from the initial feedback participant list.
- Ask the client to create the communication to stakeholders with:
    - The context and purpose for gathering feedback
    - The general nature of the coaching goals
    - An introduction of the coach
    - When the feedback process will begin
    - How the feedback will be gathered
    - What information is considered confidential
    - What information is considered anonymous
    - What the client plans to do with the feedback
    - Gratitude from the client for participating in the process

Remind Feedback Participants of the Context and Purpose

When conducting interviews or using a custom-designed survey, remind feedback participants of the context, purpose, and messages included in the invitation to participate.

Feedback participants also experience the emotional threat response based on their relationship with the client. Stakeholders in workplace or life coaching engagements may feel threatened because they are concerned about confidentiality and/or anonymity. They may hesitate to provide feedback because they do not want their relationship to change. They may fear retribution for their feedback.

Coaches can reduce the likelihood that feedback includes personal attacks or judgment about the client's identity or sexual orientation by setting the following context as the stakeholder interview begins or survey is launched:

- This is not a quiz about how much you know or don't know about the coaching client.

- You will not be asked to judge the coaching client.
- This process is not about gathering gossip or generalizations.
- Feedback questions are focused on your perspective and experiences.
- Think about interactions with the coaching client.
- Reflect on how you feel when you're working/interacting with them.
- Think of examples and real-world situations.

Reviewing Feedback with the Coaching Client

Brain-Based Feedback Reviews

Feedback reports have lots of information to review. This is another key opportunity to dampen the gay client's experiences of harassment, bullying or other unsolicited feedback. The feedback report document can be intimidating, so offer the client the following guidance to scan, examine, and internalize the feedback:

- Scan – First, scan the feedback report to get familiar with the formatting.
- Small bites – Read one section, then set it aside. Later, read another section, then set it aside.
- Sleep on it – Take advantage of the sleep cycle to process feedback.
- Highlight themes – Mark words in yellow that stand out as recurring themes or patterns.
- Highlight strengths – Mark words in green that describe strengths and favorable behaviors.
- Highlight surprises and curiosities – Mark words in orange that are a surprise or spark curiosity.
- Highlight triggers – Mark words in red that are tough to hear or trigger a defensive response.
- Insights – Write insights or realizations to bring to the next coaching session.

Coaching Gay Clients Through Feedback

Prepare the client by sharing that it may take more than one coaching session to review the feedback.

Delivering hard truths and feedback may also prompt defensive triggers for gay coaches, reminiscent of slurs, bullying, and judgement. And if the coaching client is gay, there's the risk of triggering similar experiences in them, too.

Gay coaches can dampen emotional triggers by recalling the contract and agreements they created with the client. The coach/client relationship is established, feedback questions were co-created, and guidance to review the feedback was given to the client. This is a moment for the gay coach to build their confidence by relying on their coaching expertise to dampen emotional threats that may arise.

Likewise, the gay coach can dampen emotional triggers for gay clients as the coach shares hard truths and insights in reviewing feedback. Gay clients may relive their traumas and fears of bullying and judgment as they review and summarize the feedback. Remain present, practice deep listening, and acknowledge the client's emotions.

Sharing Perspectives and Hard Truths

Coaches regularly make observations, share perspectives, and evoke awareness with coaching clients.[6] Gay coaches can use next practices in sharing observations with gay clients to dampen the client's emotionally defensive response and set aside their previous experiences when they were judged or harassed by others.

The practice is derived from Phil Dixon's research on 360 stakeholder feedback.[7] Dixon offers guidance on three types of feedback that coaches can consider as they share perspectives with clients.

1. General Personality Factors that are not actionable, not likely to change in the person, and not likely to result in improved performance. "Communicate with the team."
2. Task + Details which may be actionable, but are too specific to the feedback participant's experience, and are not likely to improve the client's performance. "Have weekly 1x1s with their direct reports with the first five minutes a review of business strategy, the next five minutes on project updates, next five minutes on customer complaints…"
3. Tasks that are actionable, allow the client to craft specific changes in their thinking and behavior, and are likely to improve performance. "Have more one-on-one meetings with direct reports."

The most effective feedback that is likely to spark insight and prompt behavior change is task-oriented feedback. When the coach makes an observation, shares perspective, or evokes awareness, frame it in the task mode to help the client determine what is possible or actionable. In the example above, the coach may share:

- What feedback sparks action?
- What did you learn that motivates a change?
- What does more one-on-one meetings with direct reports look like?
- What emotions arise when thinking about taking action?

It's not that coaches should avoid sharing all three categories of feedback. Rather, gay coaches can focus on feedback that is most likely to spark insight, shift thinking, or motivate behavior change without triggering threatening responses in the gay client's brain.[8]

While stakeholder feedback and delivering hard truths are typical elements of coaching engagements, gay coaches and gay clients may experience greater emotional threats in the feedback experience. These brain-based applications help gay coaches and gay clients engage with feedback in useful, meaningful ways while dampening emotional triggers that may detract from the coaching experience.

References

1. Dixon, P., Rock, D., and Ochsner, K., 2010, "Turn the 360 Around," NeuroLeadership Journal, Issue No. 3.
2. Inge, C., Chesebrough, C., West, T., and Rock D., 2017, "Getting to a Culture of Feedback: A science-based strategy to improve performance at scale," NeuroLeadership Journal, Issue No. 7.
3. Jung-Beeman, M., Collier, A., and Kounios, J., 2008, "How insight happens: learning from the brain," NeuroLeadership Journal, Issue No. 1.
4. Rock, D., 2008, "SCARF: A brain-based model for collaborating with and influencing others," NeuroLeadership Journal, Issue No. 1.
5. Rock, D., and Cox, C., 2012, "SCARF® in 2012: Updating the Social Neuroscience of Collaborating with Others," NeuroLeadership Journal, Issue No. 4.

6. International Coach Federation, September 19, 2021, ICF Core Competencies, https://coachingfederation.org/core-competencies.
7. Dixon, P., Rock, D., and Ochsner, K., 2010
8. Berkman, E. and Rock, D., 2014, "AIM: An Integrative Model of Goal Pursuit," NeuroLeadership Journal, Issue No. 5.

15

BEAUTIFUL GAY TEARS

By Bernie Kettle

He sobbed uncontrollably as I sat with him. Tears flowed down his cheeks, and clear mucus mixed with his tears slowly came out of his nose. Some would say not the prettiest of sights, and yet I found it beautifully raw and real.

After a while, the tears subsided somewhat. He shared his pain behind them. Having to hide being gay when growing up. Being told to hide his gayness, to figuratively not wear a sign on his forehead saying: I'm gay. Hearing all those messages about how being gay was bad, wrong, condemnable. Internalizing that and, therefore, determining while still a boy that he was bad, wrong, doomed to be damned.

Trying to overcompensate for this "flaw" by doing, doing, doing, and needing to excel at everything. Asking why God did this to him and how could God abandon him. Feeling so alone.

Believing as a teenager and a young man that there was something wrong with him because of his being gay.

Even today knowing that it isn't true, yet still believing it at some deeper, unconscious level. Seeing how he still, at times, acts from this flawed belief about himself, creating so much pain for himself, and depriving others from getting to know and fully experience the magnificence of this man.

More tears. More sobbing.

I felt honored to be in the presence of his tears. Crying in front of someone else wasn't easy for him. How could it be with the types of messages we heard as boys. Messages such as boys don't cry, don't be weak, don't show you're afraid. Particularly for a sensitive gay boy who is essentially being told to suppress the natural feminine qualities that typically show up more in boys who are gay than in straight boys.

As the tears quieted down, I sensed that there was an opening. I reminded him that he is lovable. That being gay is a beautiful part of who he is. That being gay is a gift. And that he is the amazing, powerful, magnificent man that he is because he is gay, not despite it.

More tears. Though now I could feel that these were tears of acceptance.

Gradually the wave of tears slowed and stopped. I could see a new clarity and purpose coming to him. A new resolve. He sat more upright and looked at me with clear eyes.

He decided to take action. One that would allow him to claim his gayness more boldly. That being gay is a wonderful part of who he is. In this way, he can more fully own who he is. He can allow the world to experience more of the beautiful light and soul that he is.

He had let go of some of his shame related to being a gay man through his tears. The shame that comes from being gay in a world that still tells us, in too many ways, that being gay is wrong and unnatural. He has done work around this before and he knows that he has more to do.

Yet, something shifted in him that day. In a significant way, I saw that he healed a part of himself that is needed in the healing journey of many gay men.

And…I believe that his healing contributes to the healing of the world. Whether you agree with this or not, his healing, and similar healing that other gay men experience, allows the world to benefit from a greater contribution from gay men. That, I know, is a valuable and necessary thing. That is why I work with gay men, like this one.

The way I see it, this kind of healing is about letting go the lies that we heard so often when we were younger that we believed them and internalized them—consciously and unconsciously. Those lies when still running around somewhere in our head will cause us to blend in, to hide parts of ourselves and deny others the full expression of ourselves.

When we let go of those lies, healing a part of ourselves, we each allow more of our remarkable, creative, and brilliant being to shine out. We are able to allow those gifts we have inside, the ones that we have because we are gay, to be expressed and shared more fully.

And my commitment is to create healing in the world through supporting the healing of gay men.

16

TAKING A DEVELOPMENTAL APPROACH TO COACHING GAY MEN

By F. Dominic Longo

The International Coaching Federation defines coaching as a process that inspires clients to "maximize their potential."[1] But what operating model for human potential and its realization undergirds our coaching? Are these mere clichés, like those printed over nature scenes for "inspirational" posters? As gay coaches or as coaches who support gay clients, what specific understandings do we hold for the realizable potential within ourselves or our clients?

Addressing these questions, this article sketches out some contours of the research field of adult human development (AHD) to illustrate its usefulness for coaching gay men. Along those lines, let us consider the belief that basically adults are or should be self-guided, self-motivated, and self-possessed. This expectation, common in American and other contemporary societies with various nuances, sees true adults making their own decisions and determining their own values. Adults are purported to be "achievers," with independent minds and setting the direction for their own lives. Moreover, gender politics pressures men into being (or appearing) autonomous, while women are pressured to be (or appear) socially sensitive and connected. Coaches may unconsciously bring any of these assumptions to their work with clients.

The thing is, research shows that most adults have not yet developed the complexity of mind to hold these capacities that we too commonly assume to belong to all adults.[2] Understanding and appreciating the developmental journey into and beyond this particular developmental stage or "form of mind," which psychologist Robert Kegan calls "Self-Authoring," can help us see our clients (and ourselves) with greater appreciation, understanding, and empathy.[3] For these reasons among others, gaining some acquaintance with AHD is crucial for any coach, educator, manager, or anyone supporting others to "maximize their potential."

Focusing on Gay Socialized Mind

Inquiry and reflection over the past five decades in adult human development builds on earlier research, especially Jean Piaget's work on cognitive and moral development in children. In Kegan's groundbreaking book, *The Evolving Self*, he explains being human as an activity, namely the process of evolving our meaning-making, which he calls "the doing which a human is." Among the pioneers of AHD, Kegan mentored other scholars, such as Jennifer Garvey-Berger and Susanne Cook-Greuter. Besides this emphasis on "making sense" (of self, others, and the world) as constitutive of human being, AHD demarcates stages of development by the structural complexity of the "form of mind," such as the Self-Sovereign and Socialized stages, which precede Self-Authoring, and the Self-Transforming form of mind, which comes after it.[4]

Contrary to the conventional wisdom about autonomy defining adulthood, experts regard Socialized mind as the first truly adult stage of human development. Moreover, research shows that the largest segment of adults (~50%+) are either in Socialized mind or in the transition toward Self-Authoring.[5] Even those who reach Self-Authoring (~30%) still retain Socialized mind within themselves. Like Russian dolls, each later form of mind includes (and transcends) the previous ones. Our younger, less mature forms of mind get activated in certain circumstances or take the lead in certain domains of our lives. The experience of feeling like we regress to adolescence sometimes, such as in certain interactions with our parents, speaks to this phenomenon.

While in the Self-Sovereign stage (common in adolescence and persisting for some into physical adulthood), we center on ourselves and our own basic needs. In the Socialized stage, which is variously referred to as the Conformist stage, we gain the capacity to take in external rules and the views of others. We internalize the feelings, ideas, and expectations of those others we deem important. In this way, we become "socialized," full members of social groups, for the first times in our lives. We learn how to operate in society and how to think, talk, be, and act so as to fit in.

A crucial problem arises for LGBTQ+ folks as we form a Socialized mind. Homophobia enters into us along with all of the other social material from "important others." Aversion, disapproval, even disgust for same-sex erotic love permeates the societal waters in which we swim, and this ambient homophobia of dominant society enters in and destabilizes us. Hollywood, Disney, the American Songbook, and the canon of classic literature hold up boy-girl, man-woman pairings as the ideal for all. Heteronormativity pervades culture. In fully joining society, we inevitably take into ourselves some measure of this abhorrence for same-sex attraction and love. The cultural programming that allows us to approach and eventually join the ranks of adulthood carries inside the poison pill of stigma, which for us generates self-doubt or even self-loathing. And so we "closet" and cover.

Counteracting this pervasive poisoning, we come out, latching onto some "important others" whose gender identity and sexual orientation match our own. Whether we like them or not, admire them or not, or even know them personally, we select certain LGBTQ+ folks as models and guides for the "transgressive action of embodied truth-telling" which is coming out.[6] If we are lucky or wise, we find queer peers who affirm and uphold us. Moving beyond our family of origin, we (sometimes) find our chosen family, our tribe.

Newly ensconced in tribe, whose opinions and expectations take root within us and thereby re-make our very selves, the Socialized mind adopts an "us versus them" perspective on the world and our place in it. In this affirming group of which we become a member, we find a new sense of security, the comforting embrace of "safety in numbers." Like a bee finding a hive, we gain our role, learn our place, and fit into a larger organization. We attach to one or more "Queen Bees"—important others whose implicit and explicit direction guides us and defines the right way to be and behave and work in the world.

With confidence bursting from the emboldened power of tribe, we may come to blindly reject any deviation from what we now know to be "the right way." We may see straight people to be so oblivious to sexual orientation and its very range and possibilities that they are "square, boring, cookie-cutter figures, programmed by Hollywood, dead white men, and holy books." We gays, on the other hand, may see ourselves as "enlightened, liberated, dazzlingly delightful, the very pizzazz of humanity." We glory in being the ones who create "all that is fabulous in the arts and fashion and parties." With our "queer eye for the straight guy," we might deign to "spruce up the sadly baggy suits of the straight and narrow men or the gauche style sense of unsophisticated suburban women." Indeed, reacting against stigma, we might extrapolate from our own experience and form a collectively held belief that "most straight guys (or at least the hot and smart ones!) are actually gay, but just don't know it or realize it, because they lack self-awareness. They don't yet know how good it is to be gay."

In this reactive mode of "pride tribe," gay men swarm together in an array of distinctive subgroups and communities—bears, twinks, leathermen, pigs, otters, Radical Faeries, shiny corporate gays, artsy queers, gym bunnies, bottoms and tops, femme and butch, pocket gays, muscle queens, Preppie gays, Broadway queens, and more. We become our social roles. Life might become all about getting invited to that exclusive club or having stories about the White Party. Our Fire Island share defines us, or the theme of the week we spend in Provincetown, or the queer activist group that fills our Instagram. We might live in a certain neighborhood (Bushwick? Chelsea? WeHo? Boys Town? Kreuz-kölln?), because that is "the best neighborhood."

Gay group-think empowers not only feelings of security, but of self-esteem. In harmony with the expectations of our tribe, we feel good about ourselves. We know that we matter. Socialized mind gives coherence to the self from the outside in. The power of "pride tribe" affirms our difference from the straight majority—not just setting us apart, but distinguishing us as "better," "right," "fabulous."

At the same time, seeking ongoing approval from those others whom we have deemed "ours" takes energy and attention. We chase material possessions and other status symbols, which could be Facebook "likes" as readily as a certain job title or hipster mustache. We are secretly dogged by the grip of an existential threat: the shame of exclusion from our tribe. Our very sense of self is at stake in belonging. Any disapproval from the group feels like the existential threat of being shunned, excommunicated. Were that to happen, we would not know who we are. It would feel like death.

The shadow of finding our "pride tribe" is becoming a cliché. We look outside of ourselves for our North Star to guide our trajectory in life. Our skies are filled with arrays of bright stars leading us in different directions. We might judge others by how they dress and talk, hurling easy condemnations for whatever falls outside of these norms that inhabit us. "Shoulds" hang over our every move, and we project those omnipresent obligations onto everyone else.

Working with Socialized Mind

Socialized mind holds both powerful possibilities and perilous pitfalls for gay men. As we encounter the Socialized mind in ourselves and others, we do well to appreciate just how indelibly imprinted the views, beliefs, values, and priorities of "important others" are. No defect of character or weakness of will accounts for our Socialized selves being formed by these external influences. Like any stage, Socialized mind represents a developmental triumph of evolution and expansion. The capacity to attune ourselves to others, after all, grows us far beyond the egocentric and opportunistic Self-Sovereign mind, which is befuddled by all others and left ever anxiously wondering how they might act for or against us.

We can be helpful to the Socialized minds among (and within) us by bringing attention to which "important others" they have latched onto. As coaches, we can further support our Socialized clients by listening for and amplifying their own inner voice, that self-possessed source of authority. Noticing where their own values and sense of purpose point, even when diverging from the principles, beliefs, and expectations of "important others," our clients in Socialized mind can find their way gradually to an expanded complexity of mind in which they author themselves. Growing out of Socialized mind, gay clients painfully lose the comforts of "pride tribe" and fear what can feel like a return to the lonely confusion of the Self-Sovereign stage. However, gaining autonomy, cognitive clarity, and self-possession, Self-Authoring mind marks fuller realization of human potential.

Applied specifically to gay male culture, adult human development theory can inform a coach who is wondering what "maximizing potential" might currently entail for a gay client or for ourselves. Adult Human Development can feed coaches' curiosity about what a client's (or our) growth edge might be and illuminate the various internal operating systems or forms of mind that take the lead in various situations or domains of a client's (or our own) life.

References

1. International Coaching Federation. "ICF Definition of Coaching." https://coachingfederation.org/about, Accessed 2 Jan 2021.

2. Cook-Greuter, Susanne. Nine Levels Of Increasing Embrace In Ego Development: A Full-Spectrum Theory Of Vertical Growth And Meaning Making. Prepublication version, 2013. http://www.cook-greuter.com/Cook-Greuter%209%20levels%20paper%20new%201.1%2714%2097p%5B1%5D.pdf. 2 Jan 2021.

3. Kegan, Robert. The Evolving Self: Problem and Process in Human Development. Cambridge, MA: Harvard University Press, 1982.

4. See, for example, Garvey Berger, Jennifer. Changing on the Job: Developing Leaders for a Complex World. Stanford University Press, 2012.

5. Cook-Greuter, The Nine Stages of increasing embrace in Ego Development Theory. 2013. http://www.cook-greuter.com/Cook-Greuter%209%20levels%20paper%20new%201.1'14%2097p%5B1%5D.pdf

6. Talvacchia, Kathleen T. Embracing Disruptive Coherence: Coming Out as an Erotic Ethical Practice. Eugene, OR: Cascade Books, 2019. P. 85.

17

CAN WE ACHIEVE SELF-ACTUALISATION WITHOUT BELONGING?

By Matthew Bennett

Many coaches claim to help people find their "authentic selves" or "self-actualisation." High level coaching often aims to push clients to their full potential by considering "who they can be," both in work and in their personal lives. However, there is a danger that coaches working at this level can miss deeper truths about the shaky foundations that underlie a clients' story.

This chapter will consider how two models, Maslow's hierarchy of needs and Kegan's model of Evolving Self can be used to listen for a client's deeper story to ensure that their development is safe and sustainable.[1, 2, 3, 4]

The author is a gay male coach who specialises in allowing clients to bring their full story to the table. By being explicitly non-judgmental, the author has found that clients are able to be clearer about their deep needs, and coaching can take these needs into account. This chapter draws on two case studies of clients to exemplify the how this works in practice.

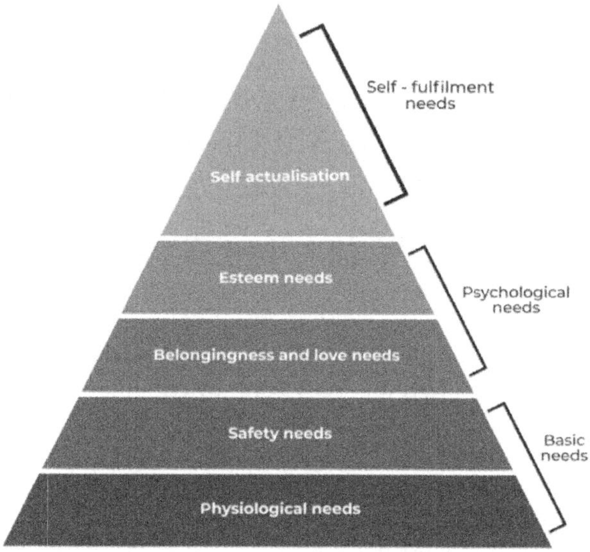

Figure 1. Maslow's Hierarchy of Needs

Maslow's Hierarchy of Needs[5]

Maslow's Hierarchy of Needs is a well-known model in psychology which suggests that humans will focus on particular categories of needs or desires only when other, more basic, needs are taken care of. For example, Maslow suggests that a person is unlikely to seek relationships before first taking care of their physiological needs such as water, food and safety.[6]

Coaches generally work with people who have their basic needs taken care of, so they are usually working at the psychological or self-fulfilment levels. In fact, many coaches claim to help their clients find self-actualisation (or similarly vaguely defined concepts such as helping clients to "find their true self," "live their best life" or "live authentically").

Kegan's Theory of Adult Development

Less well known than Maslow's theory, Kegan's Evolving Self theory suggests that adults work through a number of stages in their lives.[7, 8] The theory suggests that people move through different stages seeing themselves as "Self" (that is, their core identity) and "Object" (subject to outside factors). Kegan suggests that the more a person recognises which parts of them are "object," the more they can choose and vary their response to the environment around them, rather than being shaped by it.

Kegan's Stages of Adult Development [9, 10]

Stage	Population	Subject IS	Object HAS
1: Impulsive	(Infants)	Impulse and perception	Reflexes, senses, movement
Comment	Infants act reflexively without higher cognitive processes.		
2: Imperial	(Adolescents) 6% of adults	Needs, interests, desires	Impulses, feelings, perception
Comment	People have feelings, which they act on. Decisions are made based on perception of risk or benefit. For example, refraining from stealing because of possible consequences, not because it is "wrong."		
3: Socialized mind	58% of adults	Interpersonal relationships, mutuality	Needs, interests, desires
Comment	Adult defines themselves by a group they are in (for example political party, sports team, religion, profession). The expected norms of that group define their actions.		
4: Self-authoring mind	35% of adults	Self-authorship, identity, ideology	Relationships, mutuality
Comment	Person recognises that the emotions they feel are internal interpretations of others' actions, not caused by the other party.		
5: Self-transforming	1% of adults	IS	Self-authorship, identity, ideology
Comment	Can hold multiple thoughts and perspectives at a given point. Is not defined by a particular identity.		

What Maslow and Kegan Can Tell Us About LGBT+ Coaching Clients

Most of Western society has been built on several "in groups"—being heterosexual, cis gender, of European descent, financially stable, male, and so on. A white, cis-gender heterosexual male working in business is unlikely to have to think twice about many of the choices he makes in life because he is already part of the norm group. This is not always the case for clients who are LGBT+ or other minorities. Recognising this allows coaches to help clients overcome their barriers, moving to self-transformation (in Kegan's terminology) or self-actualisation (Maslow).

The following two case studies are drawn from the author's coaching experience and demonstrate how understanding the stage that a client is at can help them move forward. Names and minor details have been changed to protect privacy.

Case Study 1: Jeff

Jeff is a transgender male (assigned female at birth but identifies as a male). He led a sales team in a successful business. He felt prevented from further progression due to the size of the company and the fact that the company was run by a family. Most of the higher positions were held by members of the family.

Jeff's gender identity held him back from moving to a different company in a number of ways. For example, while his gender was accepted by colleagues in his current workplace, moving to another would lead to a new round of "coming out" as transgender, a process that can lead to concerns around safety and acceptance. In addition, Jeff had already found acceptance with a large group of friends in London, where he lived. His specialism meant that a new job was likely to mean moving to a different city, or even a different country. This held within it a possibility of moving to a place where there was less understanding or acceptance of trans-issues, or the support groups who fully accepted Jeff for who he was.

Through the Maslow lens, we can see that Jeff was struggling with a choice: Stay where he was, having achieved his psychological needs but unable to feel that he had fulfilled his full potential. Or risk these needs being eroded and having to reform his belongingness level in order to potentially achieve self-actualisation.

In the Kegan lens, Jeff had achieved Stage 4: The Self-authoring Mind. He was aware of his identity and ideologies and was able to draw upon relationships around him, with people whose identities and ideologies matched his own. However, his fear of moving to a different company could upset this, moving him back to Stage 3: The Socialized Mind. At this stage, Jeff would be alive to the need to develop relationships with new colleagues and new groups of like-minded individuals, with the danger of being ostracized or rejected if he did not fit into their world view.

Case Study 2: Dave

Dave was a successful businessman who was living a double life. To his work colleagues and family, he was in a long-term relationship with a woman. Secretly, he was struggling with being gay. He came to coaching to try and plot a path to leaving his girlfriend and coming out to his parents.

In a similar way to Jeff, Dave was concerned about moving from a life where he had his needs met by the life he lived, to one in which he needed to re-form all friendships in a more authentic way. In terms of Maslow, on the surface he was working on his esteem needs through his work. His story meant that he was in danger of dropping to a lower level where he needed develop new relationships before he felt able to move forward in life.

Kegan's model helps to uncover more detail on Jeff's story. Jeff was living at Stage 3 where his sense of self was dictated by the thoughts and beliefs of those around him. Throughout his coaching sessions, he was constantly preoccupied with what others would think of his actions (both past and future). By focusing on himself as the product of his relationships, he was unable to move himself forward as his whole identity was based on what and who others expected him to be.

How Coaching Moved Jeff and Dave Forward in Their Journey to Self-Actualisation

In the case of Jeff, there was a real danger of mental, physical or financial safety being put at risk by moving to a new workplace. In his case, coaching helped Jeff to separate out the various elements that he was working on at the same time. Jeff considered how to improve his career development, recognise his relationship needs, and understand the risks and benefits of moving to a different location. By the end of the coaching contract, Jeff was more aware of who he was within his world and was therefore able to plan his steps in a more resourceful way.

It became clear that Dave needed to solidify his sense of self before anything else. He was initially resistant and spent a lot of his time focusing on managing others' emotions. Over time, he came to realise that having a strong sense of being was the only way to move forward without constantly seeking the approval of those around him.

Moving Your Clients to Self-Actualisation

It is very tempting as a coach, particularly in the business, career, or executive niches, to do everything possible to drive clients to find their "best selves" or "full potential" by working at a surface level. For some clients this may be career progression, business building or improving skills in the workplace. However, sometimes it is important to delve a little deeper into a client's whole story in order to be able to ensure that the self-actualisation pyramid is not built on shaky foundations.

Coaches should be aware and receptive to areas of a clients' life that may have been ignored or papered over in order to understand them fully. Listen out for when clients are resistant to change. Consider the possibility that making changes will erode feelings of safety and security. Be ready to dig a little deeper into the client's story to help them find ways to deal with this. Sometimes, dealing with these areas may involve other modalities, such as therapy.

On other occasions, the coach being alive to the possibility that a client needs to grow as a person, to move from being dependent on others' judgements for their identity and sense of self, will help the client to move forward in life and to overcome challenges.

While it is often advised that coaches do not encourage clients to tell their stories unless they are coming from a place of resourcefulness, it is possible for coaches to use the opportunity to consider the Kegan stage of development and to use this to identify the true blockages behind a client's forward movement.

Coaches should watch for clients who define themselves only in terms of who they are to others (leader, parent), what they do for others (support, care for) or how their choices are affected by others (I have to… I must… I cannot…). These people are living at the lower adult stages of the Kegan model (aka, "Object") and can be helped by the coach to evolve upward.

Questions for coaches to consider:

How will you allow your client to open up about their full story?
How can you dig deeper to identify a client's stage of development?
How can you use this information to help them grow?
What is your stage of development?
What's keeping you from moving forward, and what in your story could move you back?
Could being more open about who you are, help your clients to open up?

References

1. Hopper, Elizabeth, Maslow's Hierarchy of needs explained https://www.thoughtco.com/maslows-hierarchy-of-needs-4582571, Accessed 21 July 2021

2. McLeod, Saul, Maslow's Hierarchy of Needs https://www.simplypsychology.org/maslow.html, Accessed 21 July 2021

3. Kegan, Robert, In over our heads, The mental demands of modern life Cambridge, London: Harvard University Press 1994

4. Morad, Natali, How to be an Adult. Kegan's theory of Adult development https://medium.com/@NataliMorad/how-to-be-an-adult-kegans-theory-of-adult-development-d63f4311b553, Accessed 21 July 2021

5. McLeod, Saul, Maslow's Hierarchy of Needs…

6. Hopper, Elizabeth, Maslow's Hierarchy of needs explained…

7. Kegan, Robert, In over our heads, The mental demands of modern life…

8. Morad, Natali, How to be an Adult. Kegan's theory of Adult development…

9. Kegan, Robert, In over our heads, The mental demands of modern life…

10. Morad, Natali, How to be an Adult. Kegan's theory of Adult development…

18

YOU SAY I CAN'T—I BELIEVE I CAN

By Peter Simmonds

The late Sir Ken Robinson—a powerful advocate for change in education due to the suppression of creativity and expression of differences among children—once gave a TED Talk called "Do Schools Kill Creativity?" He told a story of a young girl in an art class. Her teacher asked, "What are you drawing?"

"I am drawing a picture of God," she said.

"You can't draw that," replied the teacher. "Nobody knows what God looks like."

The girl looked up at her teacher with a broad smile and replied, "They will in a minute!"

This is the essence of my creative journey to becoming a coach.

When I was a kid growing up in the United Kingdom, I wasn't terribly book smart, but I loved expressing myself—by painting, cooking, and being my overall goofy and humorous self. I remember getting an A+ in Art and a B in Geography. Despite my creative talents, my teachers said, "Pete, you can't be an artist! It's not a real career choice. You should think seriously about a more academic path through geography." That advice, paired with seeing others in my family succeed and be rewarded in academia, science, and geography, set me up to betray my creative inner voice. I went to university to study environmental sciences and geography and got lost in a world that wasn't my creation. As I studied rocks and ecosystems, I longed for my creativity to be valued, but hearing you can't had silenced me and caused me to struggle to find my place in our world.

Over the years, my career didn't follow a traditional path. Other avenues opened for my creative expression working with children as a summer camp director, and I realized that I could help kids express who they were. My mission and commitment became hyper-focused on enabling others to live into their unique strengths and lead more authentic, fulfilling, and purposeful lives. The clearest decision I ever made was to become an ICF professional certified coach. I didn't think it. I felt it!

After I interviewed with several coaching firms, I heard a familiar old message. I was told, "While you are very gifted, you can't coach executives because you have no corporate experience." Well, there it was again—you can't—to which I replied, "I respectfully reject your premise. Don't corporate clients need a coach who isn't experienced in what they already know? I possess all the skills I need to coach a human, and I believe I can!" After careful consideration, one firm put their faith in me and hired me. Then my goal became real…and I thought, "Oh shit…can I really do this?"

Before my first corporate coaching meeting with a new client in April of 2019, I was extremely nervous and filled with trepidation. At that moment, I made a conscious decision. I started the meeting and said to the executive, "I just want you to know that this is the first time I am coaching a corporate executive, and I'm rather nervous. What I do know is that I'm masterfully creative at coaching a human, so we're going to be just fine." She looked at me and replied, "I love you already!"

It was a pivotal moment for me because at that moment, like many others, I realized that by being willing to embrace my fears, saying to myself, "I believe I can," and being vulnerable and transparent with her, I was truly modeling what being self-aware and authentic really looks like. She trusted me—and most of all—I trusted myself to partner as her executive coach.

As a coach, I now embody all the talents I wanted to embrace as a kid—just on a different platform. I now embrace being courageously creative: open, expressive, vulnerable, not corporate, and distinctively British. I also welcome everyone's human experience. I strongly believe in coaching from the heart by listening, being compassionate, allowing others to dream big and speak their truth, being non-judgmental, and being both provocative challenger and champion. For me, empowering people to rediscover and give voice to their truest and most hidden but inspirational self is what inspires me the most.

My personal journey of resilience to live into my creativity has only deepened my empathy and compassion for others, especially those whose voice and essence have been silenced. So, when you hear you can't, my deepest desire for you is to intentionally do what you love and live into your essence in the face of opposition and contribute to the world in every way your child-like self knows you can. Respond to those naysayers, "You say I can't—I believe I can!"

19

CONVERSATIONS WITH AN ELDER

By Brian Gorman

Our talks began casually enough. KC was the barista at Cuppa Joe, the local coffee shop. I usually stopped in during rush hour, so there were only a few sentences exchanged over the counter as he prepared the waiting orders. Over time, KC learned that I was gay and that my son, whom I had adopted out of an abusive home, was as well. I learned that he had just completed his freshman year at the local college and was working at Cuppa Joe for the summer. While he never said it, I suspected KC was gay.

The day we really talked had been a slow one at work. My calendar was clear, so I decided to head over to Cuppa Joe for a break. It was deserted except for KC, who was sitting at a table tapping away on his phone. When I walked in, he stood up, offered me a seat, and told me he would bring me my iced coffee. When he returned, I invited him to join me.

We began with the usual small talk. KC told me he enjoyed being a barista and meeting the customers. In turn, I told him a bit about my work as a coach. As sometimes happens, there was one of those awkward silences; KC seemed nervous. I asked what was on his mind. "What's it like to be gay?" he asked.

"It's different for everyone, just like being straight or bi or trans or queer or anything else. For me, being gay is now about living my life openly and authentically. For some of my friends, it's a closeted part of their lives, something that they know would hurt their spouses or children whom they love. I was married to a woman from 1972 to 1981. Back then there was no gay marriage and the LGBT community lived mostly in the shadows."

"Geez! You've lived a lot of history!"

"Soon after I came out, I picked up a gay publication and read about the discovery of a 'gay cancer' affecting men in New York City and California. It became known as Gay-Related Immune Disease or GRID; we now know it as AIDS. I was living in the Midwest and quickly became a quiet activist. I helped distribute condoms to local bars and served on the board of a lesbian and gay paper, ensuring that we published the latest news on the virus.

"In the early days, AIDS made being out even more difficult. Those diagnosed with it were treated as pariahs. Patients would be left alone in their rooms, food put down outside the door and staff afraid or unwilling to go in. In the early nineties the paradigm started to shift from dying of AIDS to living with it. By then it was clear that AIDS was not a gay-only disease, and that it would be a part of our social fabric for a long time to come."

"What was life like when you came out?"

"Which time?"

I smiled at KC's puzzled look. "Coming out is a lifelong experience. Being gay is part of who I am, not my whole identity. When I first came out, some friends accepted it and others did not. The same with family members. Back then there were few places of employment that offered protection from discrimination. As a result, in some jobs I was able to be out to most of my co-workers, and in others I was out to only one or two. These days I no longer hide the fact that I am gay. It is a tremendous feeling of freedom."

When another customer entered, KC got up to serve her with a, "Be right back." As soon as she left, he sat down again.

"I've always liked history," KC said, his nervousness gone. "But they don't teach this in school."

I chuckled. "I wasn't a history fan in school, but having lived decades of gay history, I think it's important for gay elders to share and younger generations to learn. I had a corporate job when I first moved to New York City in 1986. At the time, I was not engaging in the changing gay world. In 1990 I went to work for an AIDS organization and became active in ACT UP, the AIDS Coalition To Unleash Power. I joined picket lines and handed out condoms in front of high schools. I attended Gay Pride and served on the organizing committee."

The evening rush was starting, but before KC headed back to the counter, he proclaimed proudly, "I'm gay!" Our conversations continued throughout the summer before he went back to college. Ten years later, we continue to meet for coffee and conversation.

20

TRAINING GAY COACHES

By Dr. Damian Goldvarg

Introduction

Professional coaching training is important to assure the quality and ethical practices of professionals who call themselves coaches. In this chapter I will share my experience developing and training a program implemented at the Easton Mountain Retreat Center, near Albany, New York, targeted to gay men. I also will share comments from a survey of program graduates to learn about their experience. In the survey, I asked them to share their experiences and perspectives on the value of receiving coaching training with a specific gay group/cohort, and if gay coaching training should be different than mainstream coaching training.

Background

Training professional coaches is one of my favorite jobs. I started training coaches in 2011, when my colleague from the Center for Nonprofit Management invited me to do the first program, following the International Coaching Federation (ICF) standards. I decided to develop my training around the ICF Core Competency framework, allowing time to understand and practice the skills. In 2012, I was invited to do the same program at the University of Southern California and by organizations in Uruguay, Brazil, and companies such as Kaiser Permanente in Southern California and National Arts Strategies in Washington, D.C. I continue to run the six-month program, annually for each organization.

The Gay Coaching Professional Training covered the ICF framework comprised of eight core competencies: demonstrates ethical practice, embodies a coaching mindset, establishes and maintains agreements, cultivates trust and safety, maintains presence, listens actively, evokes awareness, and facilitates client growth.1,2 Additionally, the training included specific gay coaching issues such as coming out, HIV/AIDS, grief, and gay relationships. Participants practiced in triads, with a mentor coach providing feedback one-on-one on six coach call recordings. They also coached with five clients for twenty-five hours.

The Value of Receiving Coaching Training with a Specific Gay Cohort

After training coaches for several years, and attending International Gay Coaches Conferences, I discussed providing training for gay coaches with Harry Faddis, a founder of the Gay Coaches Alliance and a director at the Easton Mountain Retreat Center. I thought community members may benefit from building coaching skills. Also, this would offer the opportunity to coaches who had not had formal training to receive a training that would position them to be able to apply for an ICF coaching credential. Harry was enthusiastic about the idea and became the sponsor for this program.

I remember describing the project with my parents, both psychologists and coaches. They asked me, "Do you really need to do a unique program for the gay community?" I shared with them that the program would allow gay men to feel comfortable with peers, open up and build a different level of trust than in a regular program. The comments of training program participants affirmed the approach.

The Impact of Gay Coaching Professional Training for Graduate

In a post-training survey, program graduates shared poignant reflections on their experience of the impact of having training for gay men

"Training with a specific gay group created an automatic sense of trust. This trust meant that I was able to freely speak my fears, questions, and experiences to others who not only were willing to listen but able to understand. The experience was critical to my ongoing development and understanding of self." -Blake

"Studying with a group of gay men brought times of fun and camaraderie that makes room for suspending other cultural norms and simply relaxing. And we all know that relaxing makes room for greater learning." -Steven

"There is a special warmth when people want to build community around a shared identity like this. It's an entry point to finding more about what we have in common and sharing our wisdom. It also lets people use their own language more naturally—for example, to talk about their lovers, or their chosen family, or the family they don't speak to anymore." -Tucker

"Living, learning, and working with like-minded men with shared common experiences was invaluable to my coach training process. We were able to easily build a supportive community together and create a safe space for each other to share vulnerably. When receiving coach training, [it is] inevitable you are going to be working on your own personal growth. When you are doing that in a deep and meaningful way, it can be a very exposing, sometimes uncomfortable, and sometimes even scary process. Having that quickly developed support system in place was invaluable." -Wil

"As gay men, most of us have spent some portion of our lives hiding parts of ourselves. Coming out of the closet is a life-long experience as we meet new people and form new personal and professional relationships. When we arrived at the training, we were out to one another by virtue of being there. That alone created a common foundation for relationships to build. Before our training even began, community was forming. My triad, which formed in March of 2016 as our training began, is still meeting every two weeks five years later. As gay men, each of us brought with us our own stories and experiences which allowed us to teach one another about topics that would remain unaddressed (or might even be taboo) in other coach training programs: being a long-term AIDS survivor, the challenges of being a gay senior, coming into oneself through drag, etc." -Brian

Should Gay Coaching Training be Different from Mainstream Coaching Training?

Comments from program graduates affirmed the importance of this training focus and approach:

"The benefit of gay coaching training provides the needed space to discover and claim a healthy sense of self-worth and to explore what it means to build healthy relationships. I live and work in a community that affirms the value and participation of LGBTQIA people. Yet, even in an affirming environment, the willingness and/or ability of straight allies to allow for deeper conversations and understanding remains an obstacle. Recently I challenged a straight ally who asked 'Why should anyone care what you do in your bedroom?' This dismissive, reductionistic question is common. 'But you're missing so much of who I am when you say that,' I replied. 'You are only seeing part of who I am. There is far more about me than what I do in my bedroom. Yes, I have a sexual preference, but I also have an identity that comes with a particular personality, a way of communicating and processing emotions and information.' " -Blake

"I can speak for myself that the gay focused coaching training gave me the needed space to discover my fuller identity and to hone my gifts in a safe, trusting environment."-Blake

"I prefer to separate coach training from gay coach training. The ideas, principles and practices for coach training are pretty clear. The norms for good practices are what are important to learn in any coach training. However, gay coach training is a bonus and should create an option to explore and build expertise pertinent and specific to the gay community. An example: The current science of helping others underscores how the brain works under stress and when calm—that needs to be taught in all coach training. Developing awareness, tools and practices that recognize what impacts stress and calm to clients from the gay community can be a uniquely important toolset." -Steven

"I believe gay coach training should incorporate education around challenges that are specific to the gay experience. When supporting LGBTQ folks, it's important to have an awareness and understanding of what specific issues that demographic may have struggled with in the past or are currently struggling with. A comprehensive gay coach training programs needs to thoroughly and completely cover all the standard elements of a coach training, and then in addition to that also offer aspects of education and training that are specific to working with LGBTQ folks... While we were as serious as I am sure most coach trainees are, the all-gay environment also allowed for playfulness, whether it be showing up to class in heels or, a drag night, or storytelling. The location of our training, Easton Mountain, also offered unique opportunities for relaxing and bonding in nature, in the hot tub, in the sauna, and in the sunroom." -Wil.

"Each of us belongs to many sub-cultures; none of us should be defined by just one. Being gay isn't all that is important about me, and it is an important part of who I am. For thirty-one years I lived as a heterosexual male; starting in my teens when I realized my difference, I lived in the closet. As a gay man, I understand 'different.' I have hidden my identity, sometimes even from myself. I have lived as an outsider. And, I have learned both the challenges and the importance of living fully, authentically, into oneself. The coming out journey, while different in many ways for each of us, allows those of us who are gay coaches to bring a deeper understanding to many of our clients' most significant challenges."-Brian

"People live out gay identity in different ways. Being gay can be tied to relationships and friendships and community action, or it can be more of a private feeling. For some men, having sexual partners is an important part of their gay or bi experience, while others spend a lot of time single and not necessarily seeking companionship. Also—this is a different thing—some men feel part of a community that recognizes their gender and sexuality and gives them opportunities to talk and to learn from others like them, while others haven't 'found their people' and may not feel much a drive to seek out community. It's helpful to know how these kinds of connections might be affecting someone's happiness and self-worth." -Tucker

Conclusion

Based on comments from graduates shared above, we can confirm the value of a training space where people were able to be themselves with other gay men, and created space that enhanced the possibility to be authentic, supported, and respected. The program allowed participants to be fully themselves and learn from each other in a fun and relaxed atmosphere, surrounded by the beauty of nature at the Easton Mountain Retreat Center.

I suggest that other affinity groups, especially those who are historically oppressed or stigmatized, might find similar benefit from focused coach training. I hope in the future the gay coaching program will be implemented again, providing this important opportunity to others in LGBTQ+ communities.

References

1. International Coach Federation Coaching Competency Framework https://coachingfederation.org/core-competencies.
2. Goldvarg, D, Mathews, P, Perel N.: Professional Coaching Competencies. The Complete Guide. 2018. Executive College Press.

21

YEAR ONE OF COACHING AND A LIFETIME OF CHANGE

By Cator Sparks

What a wondrous journey coaching training has been. Through it, I have been completely rewired.

When I first started this journey, I was in such a different place. I was at a pretty low point and that's why I decided to really stop to rethink my life and what I wanted. I love listening and watching people blossom, and life coaching has helped me tremendously over the past nine years, so I asked around to therapists I knew and even my own coach about their thoughts of me exploring this career move. They all cheered me on like they had been waiting for me to make this decision since birth. Their response was my first boost of confidence on my new adventure.

Looking back through my notes, sitting with all I have been reading, listening to, learning, I wanted to reflect on some of the bigger picture concepts I have learned through my first year of coaching:

- Slowing down: From the moment I wake up, I make sure to take a few minutes just for me, in silence, for my thoughts to come into form and not instantly reaching for my phone.
- Flow: The way I talk to people has changed. I ask empowering questions in everyday dialogue. I listen deeper. I try to let go of judgment.
- Listening: I now can tap into my three levels of listening and really see the meta-view (big picture) instead of focusing on the minutia. This also has strengthened my intuition, which is a big part of coaching.
- Pride: Anyone who has read *The Velvet Rage* has most likely worked on their "Gay Shame," but it wasn't until coaching that

I really dug into this. I was usually the only gay person in the class so talking openly about being bullied, "sounding gay," and finding power in my drag persona was life changing. I've always thought of myself as a proud gay man, but focusing on my values, life purpose, and inner allies, I really took my pride and acceptance of myself to another level.

- Truth: The biggest lesson I have learned is speaking my truth. I have spent years being talked down to and not standing up for myself—in jobs, relationships, and friendships. I never want to hurt anyone or rock the boat. And that has caused me to be bulldozed and bullied.
- Go Deep: I have learned to deepen the learning and not forward the action quite so fast. A life coach is not there to tell a client what to do. The answers come from the client and you just guide them along with the right questions. We don't have to solve any issues by the end of a call, we can go deep and let the client marinate in it until the next call.
- I have learned that there are parts of me that may not ever change. But how I handle those demons has changed, from numbing them with alcohol to calming them through meditation, yoga, kettlebells, and the power of positive thinking.
- Coaching skills are life skills. I love sharing what I have learned with my clients so they too can live a life that is more balanced, that flows.

Self-work is never done. It's an ongoing process for those who choose to accept the challenge. I have gained so much self-confidence, self-love, patience, and acceptance through this journey. I am excited to share all of this knowledge with clients, friends, and family. I am also thrilled to be in a profession where the learning never ends. I am facilitating a GBTQ+ men's group every Wednesday for the national men's organization, EVRYMAN, as well as coaching for Boon Health, a mental health platform. Also, being a part of The Gay Coaches Alliance has helped me network with other gay coaches and even try some of their programming.

I am ready for the next chapter to unfold. I am excited to see where the next year takes me and this new career path. I am trying so hard to be patient. But I am eager to expand my business, connect with more clients, and continue to learn and grow in the wellness world. Even coaches have to coach themselves: I know I simply need to take a deep breath, connect to self and spirit, and keep my eye on the prize.

22

THE BLURRED LINE: COACHING OR THERAPY?

By Matthew Bennett

There are many different forms of therapy. The terminology used for therapy and therapists can vary greatly, depending on laws of particular jurisdictions, accrediting bodies, licences, and ability to prescribe drugs. In this chapter, "therapy" and "therapist" are used to cover all types of counselling and psychotherapy that would fall under the remit of various professional bodies, e.g., the American Psychological Association, American Counseling Association, British Association for Counselling and Psychotherapy or similar. "Coaching" and "coach" are used for professionals whose work would fall under the remit of various bodies in many countries, the largest example being The International Coaching Federation (ICF).

There have been many attempts to distinguish the difference between coaching and therapy. In some contexts, the distinction is clear and unambiguous. A client approaching a coach for coaching to "overcome suicidal ideation" or "get over childhood trauma" is clearly in need of therapy rather than coaching. Likewise, a client approaching a therapist for "an action plan to start a business" or "to develop the best response to an underperforming employee" would be best referred to a coach.

However, there are times where the distinction becomes more blurred, in particular, in life coaching or in coaching an LGBT+ client whose challenges in business stem from complications drawn from their sexuality, or gender identity. The boundary of when to refer these clients to another modality becomes more nuanced.

Initial coach training frequently emphasises a form of wording that suggests that answers within coaching should come from within the client and that the client should be seen as "whole," "okay," or "well-functioning." Other modalities can be employed when a client does not have internal resources to overcome a particular issue, and many coaches are comfortable moving between modalities as required. For example, many coaches would be willing to offer a client a piece of information, model, or theory in order to help them overcome a challenge if the client did not appear to have these resources. Let's say a client could tell their coach that they did not know how to performance manage their team. Many coaches would be comfortable offering a number of different models of performance management that could suit the client and allow the client to build on those models.

Many modalities of therapy, on the other hand, start with the assumption that patients have a "disorder" that needs to be "cured," although terminology for this varies considerably and is actively discussed and disputed. The fundamental starting point is often that the client is "abnormal," "unhealthy" or in some other way "broken" and requires "fixing."

LGBT+ individuals have sometimes fallen foul of this system of classification of "normal" verses "abnormal." Homosexuality and gender dysphoria have both been classified as mental illnesses in the past.1 Similarly, some fetishes have at various times been pathologized.[1,2]

It may be possible that coaches who openly identify as gay or part of the LGBT+ continuum are more likely to find that their clients are willing to be more open about aspects of their lives. These clients may be less open with coaches who downplay their sexuality or gender identities. The author has often noticed that there is an assumption of a shared history and understanding of the world among gay men. This has manifested in a number of ways. For example, discussion of non-monogamous relationships is more common with gay men, as are references to sexual activities within professional conversations. For coaches, this could mean that a coach is more likely to uncover issues outside of the original contracted remit.

As an example, the author recently coached a client who was feeling lost in their career. The client was a dancer in theatre and had achieved considerable success. He had achieved all of the goals he had set himself and was trying to decide what to do next. After a few career-focused sessions, he confided that he had a self-diagnosed sex addiction which he stated was preventing him from moving forward. He was spending more time looking for casual sexual encounters than working on the activities that would lead him to the next step in his career.

Many coaches would see this as a cut-and-dry case where the client needed to be referred to therapy. However, it is worth considering whether this is actually the case. To immediately stop coaching and refer the client to therapy suggests that the coach has made a number of assumptions and judgements: that the client was "not okay," that the challenge is (likely to be) a diagnosable problem, and that the challenge actually prevented moving forward in the client's journey to career satisfaction. Jumping to conclusions like this can cause a lot of harm and add to client feelings of being judged, compounding the problem. An additional consideration is that most coaches are not trained or qualified to make a psychological diagnosis.

If, instead, the client had presented with the same history but suggested that his challenge was that he spent too much time exercising at the gym, then the challenge would likely be viewed in a completely different way. In this case, many coaches would try a "wheel of life" approach, considering how much time the client was taking up with different activities, and how best to find balance in life by reducing the time taken for activities that were not moving him forward toward his goals.[3]

There are some situations (for example suicidal ideation, inability to function normally, self-harm or abuse of others) where a coach must refer a client, referred to in the ICF Code of Ethics in section 4.[4]

> 8. Remain alert to indications that there might be a shift in the value received from the coaching relationship. If so, make a change in the relationship or encourage the Client(s)/Sponsor(s) to seek another coach, seek another professional or use a different resource.

However, there are also situations in the grey area. The key to deciding what to do next comes from a partnership model of coaching.[5]

The first, and most important step is to reiterate the boundaries of coaching, and to ensure that the client and coach are clear about the experience and abilities of the coach. Most coaches who do not have formal training in therapy are unable to "fix" disorders using the skill sets taught by coach training. However, coaches are very used to asking questions that can circumvent problems.

Questions that a coach could ask might include:

- If you didn't have that problem, what would you do?
- What are some ways you could avoid the issues that that problem causes?
- Is that actually the issue here, or are you using it to mask another issue?
- Given that you have this problem, what other options do you have?

If the issue truly stops progress, then it's highly likely that the client needs to be referred to a therapist to deal with the issue before continuing the coaching relationship. At other points it may be appropriate to set particular challenges aside and work on different areas of a client's life or give the client time to work with a therapist at the same time as a coach. It is recommended that the coach, the client, and the therapist all be transparent about agreement on working arrangements.

It may be useful to consider a physical illness as an example here. If a client had broken their leg, then it would be right for a coach to suggest that the client should work with a doctor or physiotherapist to heal the broken leg. As a partnership, it would then be legitimate to decide whether using coaching to discuss starting a new business as a freelance gardener was something that was worth working on, or, whether the client should put the contract on hold until their leg was better. Some clients would value the time with a coach to plan the business, discuss marketing and so on. Whereas others could wish to hold back until their leg was healed before moving forward. Still others could ask to use coaching to find ways to garden while they were unable to walk properly.

In the case of the dancer who was "addicted" to casual sex discussed above, the author as coach and the client decided that it was important to address the "addiction" to casual sex before moving forward with his career goals (note, it is not for a coach to diagnose an addiction).

In other cases, the author has successfully coached clients to achieve their goals even though they have been diagnosed by a qualified professional with disorders such as PTSD, depression or childhood trauma. In the case of the first two diagnoses, the clients were working with therapists in parallel with coaching. In the case of the client with childhood trauma, the client had decided that they were not at a point in their life in which they wished to delve into the issues, but they were able to consider future possibilities while avoiding the specific problems that arose from it. In each of these cases, the clients were well aware of their current situations and the challenges they faced. Their mental health issues were present but circumvented wherever possible. Examples of this could be to avoid triggering situations, planning work to allow for mental health breaks, or including others in wider care plans while focusing on particular goals and challenges in coaching.

Some initial coach training often tells new coaches that they should avoid discussion of the past. More nuanced training sometimes changes this to "discuss the past if there are resources that can be used in the present or future." With regard to issues that could require therapeutic assistance to overcome, perhaps this should be changed to "if an issue from the past is causing challenges in the present, the coach and client should discuss whether they can learn from, or avoid, this challenge, or whether the client needs to be referred to a therapist to deal with the challenge." The coach can add great value by partnering with the client to envision their best way forward and appropriate resources.

Coaches who work in the space where they may be confronted with mental health issues should be alive to their own judgements and biases. As soon as a coach starts to believe that a client is incapable of doing something because the client is "mentally ill," it becomes unlikely that the coach will be able to effectively partner with the client as they do not believe that they are resourceful enough to progress. Under these circumstances, it is important to admit that the coaching relationship is not going to be successful and to work with the client to find a better way to solve the problem.

The checklist below may help you to make decisions on whether to refer a client to a therapist.

Client Referral Checklist

Question	**Suggestion**
Is the client's issue interfering with their ability to carry out everyday tasks such as feeding themselves, going to work or normal leisure activities?	If so, it is likely that the client needs to be referred.
Does the issue pose an immediate and significant risk of injury or death to the client or other people?	This must be addressed by involving the relevant authorities or helping the client make contact with relevant agencies.
Does replacing the issue with a "benign" issue change your view of the need for referral?	If changing the issue to "the client has a broken leg" or "the client watches too much television" or similar changes your view, the true issue may with your judgement. To expand, compare the two following scenarios: • My client spends too much time being spanked. • My client misses work because she is constantly searching for new sexual partners. Replacing 'being spanked' with 'watching television' suggests that coaching could be used. The second example would suggest a compulsion that may require therapeutic help.
Do you feel that the problem is more than you can handle, outside your area of expertise, is triggering for you, or concerns you in any other way?	It will be difficult for you to partner with the client and you should recognise this and refer the client on.
Does the issue need to be addressed for the client to move forward in their coaching challenge?	If so, temporarily suspending coaching, or changing to a different challenge while the client works on the issue with a therapist may be appropriate.
Can the issue be circumvented or simply taken into account?	If so, the client may not need therapy.

The International Coaching Federation Booklet, *Referring a Client to Therapy: A Set of Guidelines*, goes into more detail on this subject and should be consulted if in doubt.[6]

References

1. American Psychological Association, Task Force on Appropriate Therapeutic Responses to Sexual Orientation. (2009). Report of the American Psychological Association Task Force on Appropriate Therapeutic Responses to Sexual Orientation. Retrieved from http://www.apa.org/pi/lgbc/publications/therapeutic-resp.html accessed 16 July 2021.
2. Psychology Today 2019 Fetishistic Disorder https:"www.psychologytoday.com/us/conditions/fetishistic-disorder, Accessed 16 July 2021.
3. Sutton, J 2020 How to apply the wheel of life in coaching https://positivepsychology.com/wheel-of-life-coaching/, Accessed 16 July 2021.
4. ICF 2019 ICF Code of Ethics, international Coach Federation https://coachfederation.org/code-of-ethics, Accessed 4 January 2021.
5. Cory, D and Bradley, R 2018 Partnership Coaching https://thesystemsthinker.com/partnership-coaching/, Accessed 16 July 2021.
6. ICF 2018 Referring a Client to Therapy: A Set of Guidelines, International Coach Federation https://coachfederation.org/app/uploads/2018/06/Whitepaper-Client-Referral-June-2018.pdf?inf_contact_key=602b4d59a1a0c7314b8b6b2f7da46743e5b9ba877dc809a5f95407026ca0684b, Accessed 4 January 2021.

23

PEER COUNSELING: COACHING SERVICES AS AN LGBTQ COMMUNITY CENTER OFFERING

By S. Mark Kennedy

A young lesbian woman struggles to share her sexual orientation with the religious family that she loves deeply. A middle-aged man in a traditional marriage fears the impact coming out will have on his family and is terrified of losing his children. A young trans adult seeks emotional support and resources as they grapple with transitioning decisions. An elderly, home-bound adult struggles with isolation and loneliness. A gay man in recovery struggles with housing insecurity after being thrown out by his partner. These are just a few of the struggles presented by clients connecting with the Peer Counseling Program at William Way Community Center, an LGBTQ center located in Philadelphia's famous Gayborhood.

Peer Counseling is a frontline, direct service that provides free, short-term (up to twelve sessions), goal-oriented coaching to the LGBTQ community and beyond.[1] The service, offered by phone or in-person, is anonymous, confidential and sex-positive creating a highly approachable, low anxiety way to start the process of resolving stressful life situations and empowering clients. The anonymity creates a safe space to discuss sensitive topics such as coming out, gender identity, transitioning, sexuality and sexual practices, immigration status, dating, loneliness, living with HIV, relationship issues, religion, cultural issues, financial insecurity and beyond. When clients call/visit, they encounter Peer Counselors (PCs) who are engaged, non-judgmental, and genuinely caring.

LGBTQ individuals often experience an extra layer of complexity required to navigate societal attitudes/prejudices and a lack of LGBTQ legal protections.[2] Since the PC staff identifies as LGBTQ+, PCs are able to appreciate that context and complexity because of their own lived experience. This allows PCs to access both empathy and awareness easily to coach clients more effectively. Consequently, clients will often talk about issues they've never spoken about out loud.

While the program is called Peer Counseling in order to reach clientele in an understandable way, it is actually a coaching program. We found that coaching is a less well understood term in general than counseling. Therapy seeks to bring unconscious motivations as interpreted or diagnosed by a mental health professional to consciousness via specific therapeutic methods. PCs do not offer therapy or advice and refer mental health issues to professionals. Instead, they actively listen to each client, ask open-ended questions to help the client clarify the situation, catalyze self-awareness to generate options, empower the client to create an action plan, and offer a point of ongoing support and accountability as the client implements their plan.[3,4] The PC may offer referrals to vetted, LGBTQ-affirming support groups, social programs, and legal and health practitioners.

This Peer Counseling program serves a highly diverse clientele in a large metropolitan area. Clients each bring a beautiful, intricate, unique and complex intersectionality of gender identity, sexual orientation, race, culture, economic status, and other social affiliations. PCs are mindful that each client's world experience is unique. PCs understand that they will never be fully competent at someone else's intersection, but they can take on a humble mindset to listen and learn the client's perspective without assumptions. This encourages PCs to refrain from advising and become aware of their own discomfort points so these are not misperceived as judgment.

Typical Session

As an anonymous service, the client provides only a first name in response to the question, "What would you like me to call you?" This allows clients exploring their gender identity to experiment with a name that matches their true identity, often the first opportunity to do this in a safe environment. It also allows clients concerned about anonymity to use pseudonyms. Clients may also request a PC of a specific gender identity, sexual orientation, race, etc. to increase comfort.

The PC begins to establish a rapport with the client and invites the client to share the purpose of their call/visit. This critical early juncture requires radical presence and openness. Clients are often sharing challenges and parts of themselves never before shared. Intense expressed emotions are common as clients may have contacted Peer Counseling due to a triggering life event. The ability of the PC to listen actively and exude presence, authenticity and caring allows the PC to build trust with the client. The PC will use tools such as reflecting feelings, summarizing, and paraphrasing both to demonstrate their attentiveness to the client and request feedback on the accuracy of what was heard. For walk-ins, body language is also critical to the communication of connection and empathy.

Once a client has indicated that their content, context and emotions feel heard, the PC encourages the client to explore and clarify the challenge through open-ended questions, reframing, direct communication, and gently confronting inconsistencies all while continuing to express empathy, exude presence and listen actively. The goal is to create awareness as a basis to explore options using standard coaching practices.[5]

As a client explores options to meet their challenge, the PC may use "what else?" questions to encourage creative options and silence to give time for thoughts and connections to emerge in the client. As the client creates their preferred options, the PC encourages the client to divide the options into actionable tasks and to set goals. The PC may offer community resources useful in achieving goals and will, at the request of the client, provide contact information for those vetted resources.

Sessions typically end with a client commitment regarding an actionable goal, creating both client accountability and an agreement on the need and timing for a next session. Words of encouragement close the session on a note of continued rapport. Demographic metrics are generally collected at this time. These basic demographic metrics allow the Center and its funding agencies to better understand the communities being served, and the metrics also help the peer counseling program identify underserved communities to improve outreach and advertising efforts.

After the session, the PC will write a brief DAP (data/assessment/plan) note. These notes are strictly confidential (available only to PCs) and allow the PC to track client progress.

As a client approaches their final gratis sessions, the PC

collaborates with the client to transition their continuing longer-term work to a professional coach and/or therapist.

PC Selection and Training

Potential new PCs self-nominate and are interviewed by a team of experienced PCs. Candidates are selected for their ability to listen actively, empathize, maintain presence, and remain open and affirming, having also demonstrated an ability to effectively address challenges in their own lives.

Candidates are provided with intensive training before assignment. Training begins with commitment to the ethical standards of the program: client anonymity, client confidentiality, non-fraternization with clients, and avoidance of leading/advising (except in the case of safer sex practices).

Training includes communication (active listening; impact of voice intonation, pitch, tone, and volume; body language), basic coaching skills, specific commonly encountered topics, and crisis management (suicide assessment and prevention, clients under the influence of substances, personal safety with walk-in clients). Much of the training is experiential involving group exercises, personal sharing and role plays. Role plays are a critical and substantial component of the training. Training participants and experienced PCs observe the role plays and offer constructive feedback to be practiced in subsequent role plays. Role play topics are selected from generalized examples of frequently encountered client challenges. Consequently, they prepare candidates not only in coaching methodology, but also in the specific topics they are most likely to encounter.

New PCs are then assigned to shifts and role plays continue for at least four weeks during the shift. Experienced PCs will share synopses of sessions to give new PCs ideas for approaching various client challenges. The shift leader in consultation with the new PC decides when a new PC may begin taking client calls based on new PC comfort level and a personalized skills assessment.

Ongoing PC Support

Individual PCs receive ongoing support. A shift leader is assigned to each shift. The shift leader manages logistics and provides care and support to the PCs on that shift. This may take the form of providing resource referrals and answering questions during a call, providing emotional support after a tough session, assisting with emergencies and maintaining a safe environment.

There is a monthly supervision and training meeting for all volunteers in the program. The group as a whole can provide emotional support, discuss alternative approaches to difficult issues, and surface new resources. Supervision is provided by a licensed, doctoral-level clinical psychologist available at monthly meetings and for urgent emotional support and case discussions as needed. Monthly meetings also assess cases that may require mental health referrals. Monthly training keeps PCs updated on community and national resources as well as current terminology and practices. Example training topics include gender identity, community resources (youth, legal, homelessness, support groups, faith groups), health, relationship dynamics, and teambuilding. A program coordinator oversees the operation of the program, conducts a monthly shift leader meeting designed to assess the well-being of each shift's PCs, and is available to talk individual PCs through issues or struggles.

Program Administration

The program runs on a shoestring budget. A volunteer workforce staffs and runs the program. William Way Community Center provides private meeting space, phone lines, basic website advertising, and basic needs (e.g., copying). Additional advertising occurs through social media and regional Pride events. Such a program can be very affordable to implement and administer. Decisions in the program are made by consensus within the PC volunteer community.

Outcomes

The program collects very basic demographic information if (and only if) a client is willing to share information. Through this the program learns the diversity of clients served which can be used for insights into future outreach, development and training, and additional funding. More important are the client outcomes expressed verbally or captured in the DAP notes. The host of successful outcomes for clients coming out, transitioning, managing relationships, connecting with people, and accepting and enjoying themselves speak to the magic of active listening, empathy, genuine interest and caring, affirming engagement, and resource availability that the PC coaching provides. This program may only be the beginning of a journey for some clients, but engaging a client in an experience of lovingkindness can be the spark that encourages transformation in the life of a client to live more consciously and authentically in a world that can be difficult to navigate for the LGBTQ community.

The Peer Counseling Program at William Way Community Center could serve as a model of a coaching service to the LGBTQ community and beyond, that brings frontline, direct coaching services to clients regardless of financial means. Other municipalities nationwide are encouraged to develop similar programs or connect with the program at William Way to utilize the services provided.

To speak with a peer counselor, go to www.waygay.org/peer for the current access number. To speak more about the content and structure of the program or for potential collaborations, contact the author via his Coach profile on the GCA website: thegaycoaches.com.

References

1. William Way LBGT Peer Counseling, www.waygay.org/peer, accessed January 20, 2021.
2. Roland, C. B. & Burlew, L. D. (Eds.), 2017, Counseling LGBTQ Adults Throughout the Life Span, Retrieved from https://www.counseling.org/docs/default-source/default-document-library/counseling-lgbtq-adults-throughout-the-life-span-final.pdf?sfvrsn=2
3. International Coach Federation, April 2018, "Referring a Client to Therapy: A Set of Guidelines", https://coachingfederation.org/app/uploads/2018/06/White paper-Client-Referral-June-2018.pdf
4. California Association of Marriage and Family Therapists, July 2015, https://coachingfederation.org/blog/new-icf-resource-helps-coaches-understand-when-and-how-to-refer-clients-to-therapy

5. Watson, Judith & Gislason, Michelle, Coaching Skills for Nonprofit Managers and Leaders, San Francisco: Jossey-Bass, 2010.

24

THE QUARBI+ SIX-PHASE APPROACH TO COACHING QUEERS

By James A. Lopata

When I give keynotes on Diversity, Equity, and Inclusion (DEI), I stand comfortably in front of the audience, wearing a suit jacket, pressed shirt, khakis, and Kenneth Cole shoes. I ask the audience what they see.

"A guy with a great smile," says one.

"Why thank you," I acknowledge.

"A middle-aged white dude," says another.

"A skinny white dude," adds another.

"Someone who looks like you work in corporate America," says one.

"I presume you're cis-gender male and straight," adds another.

"Interesting," I respond.

"What's cis-gender?" asks an audience member.

"Born male and identifies as male," shouts someone.

And on.

Then I acknowledge that they are probably wondering why a white, middle-aged corporate man is giving a keynote on DEI.

I hear a loud dismissive, "Uh-huh."

I go on and tell them that when I look in a mirror, I see everything they have mentioned—a white, middle-aged, corporate guy. But when I look more deeply into my eyes, I see a scared little gay kid who loved skipping through school hallways singing show tunes, who was made of fun of because of it, had his books dumped on the ground, and was beat up.

I see a small, frightened queer boy who learned early that it wasn't safe to be himself. I learned to hide aspects of my personality. In DEI, we say that I learned to "cover." As RuPaul says, "We're born naked, and the rest is drag." I donned corporate drag for decades.

I began working right on Wall Street in lower Manhattan long before there were Employee Resource Groups (ERG) in companies for LGBTs or other minority populations. In fact, the term LGBT had not yet been coined. We were gays and lesbians. And we hid.

Gradually, we came out and expanded our impact. We did so in a rough chronology that I summarize in six phases that create an acronym "QuARBI-plus." We began in (1) Quiet. Slowly we found each other on the sly, and we formed what we called (2) Affinity Groups at work, where we'd meet in secret and support each other by sharing how we survived homophobia and fag jokes in the workplace. As we gained confidence, some of us asked for formal acknowledgement by our companies and we organized into (3) Employee Resource Groups ("ERG"), with explicit support from management, helping integrate and make others like us feel safe at work. Soon, ERGs became (4) Business Resource Groups ("BRG"), which were provided additional budgets to connect with customers and make a difference in business growth. As our confidence and influence grew, we brought more of our full selves and talents to work, which increased (5) Innovation. Today, we are expanding to (6) add systemic intersectionality (Plus) with other minority groups to increase our impact.

What does this have to do with coaching? There is a fairly standard construct for leadership development that is used in many corporate coaching environments, which uniquely aligns with these six phases of corporate integration for Queer People in the workplace. The framework generally consists of categorizing competencies in a few buckets, such as "leading self," "leading others," "leading change," and so on. At AceUp, where I serve as Vice President of Coaching Supervision, we classify our competencies into four areas: Leading Self, Leading Others, Leading Organizations, and Leading Change.[1] For QuARB+, I add a prelude phase, the Starting Point, and a postlude phase, Leading Beyond. Here is a full summary of this QuARBI+ Six-Phase Approach:

(1) **Q**uiet, the Starting Point, often the gay employee's starting point, from which we make sure no one knows we are queer.

(2) **A**ffinity, or Leading Self, where we begin to lead ourselves out of hiding and into a safer space to begin to show up more confidently.

(3) **R**esource, or Leading Others, where we begin to help others like us who aren't as far down the confidence path as we are.

(4) Business Resource, or Leading Organizations, where we align our unique identity to help build business in ways that others in our company can't.
(5) **I**nnovation, or Leading Change, which expands on the leading organizations, where we bring an even greater use of our gifts to bear on innovation and change management for all stakeholders in our company for better.
(6) **P**lus, or Leading Beyond, where we truly begin to break barriers between us and anyone else.

As a Coach, I work with queer clients in this QuARBI+ opening up process.

(1) Quiet. The Starting Point. One queer person I coached who worked at a large bank, relayed a story about why being quiet can be the right thing to do. He shared an anecdote about when he entered the workforce as a young sales professional. At one of the first team meetings he attended, his boss told everyone, "Look, you guys need to fucking deliver. Oh, and if any of you faggots are offended by my language, you can just pack up and leave now." So, you learn to be quiet, just to keep your job. Or you walk out. At this point, coaching is about helping to build awareness about possibilities. It's about helping the queer person begin to move to the second level, Leading Self.

Key coaching questions I like to ask clients in these situations are: How comfortable are you here? What are other options? How okay are you with staying in this situation? What would it take for you to leave? Where can you turn to for additional assistance?

(2) Affinity. Leading Self. When someone begins to be open to looking elsewhere, and that can mean even including a coach in discussions, the client begins to lead themselves. This is critical. In affinity with others like themselves, including, say, with a gay or queer coach, coachees begin to see more possibilities. They can build confidence in their abilities to move forward. They may still hide their true identities in the workplace, but they can begin to see a better way forward.

Possible coaching questions for phase two include: What do you see others doing that inspire you? How might an ideal future for you look in a year or two?

(3) Resource. Leading Others. In the chronology of DEI

development, this was the phase where Human Resources (HR) and recruiting began to notice that companies could attract great talent if, say, all things being equal with two job offers, a gay person found out that one company had a gay and lesbian ERG and the other did not. HR would leverage employees who were comfortable being fully out at work to help meet with potential employees and others.

In coaching in this third phase, I might ask questions like: How might you leverage your identity for greater good? How can you create more leadership possibilities for yourself as an out queer person?

(4) Business. Leading the Organization. This is where we start to make big inroads. I once coached a transgender man who was very active in his corporate LGBT ERG and he helped many others. This man also did great work in his regular job and was promoted regularly. Every year he wrote some of what he was doing with the LGBT Business Resource Group (BRG) into his performance review. And every year, his boss would delete it from the evaluation, arguing that BRG work wasn't important for the business. When I was coaching the young man in a specially designed leadership development course for LGBT leaders, the employee was able to make a strong case that, indeed, the work he did for the BRG, held real value for the firm. Because of his work in helping people in the sales department communicate more genuinely with transgender customers, he directly helped create more revenue for the firm.

Coaching queries at this phase might include: How is what you're doing connected to your customers? How is it aligned with other business stakeholder initiatives? How is your ability to be out and help others making greater impact? How can you better promote your unique contributions in the workplace? Think big.

(5) Innovative. Leading Change. The example I use a lot in this phase is one where Chief Justice John Roberts famously asked in a 2015 affirmative action case: "What unique perspective does a minority student bring to a physics class?" Rhetorically speaking, when you're working in abstract sciences, what does anyone's skin color, or, by extension, sexual orientation, have to do with the topic? A few days later, Jedidah C. Isler, PhD, a Black astrophysicist, answered Roberts in an op-ed in The New York Times.2 Particularly in the abstract sciences, she argued, diverse representation is essential. For example, we can't see quantum mechanics with the naked eye. We understand quantum mechanics through metaphor.

In fact, the quantum term "quark" comes from Irish literature, from James Joyce's novel Finnegan's Wake. Cultural references anchor metaphors that help us understand what we can't see. Diverse ways of seeing enhance and accelerate innovation.

Coaching questions for this phase may include: What can your unique perspective bring to the table? What are you seeing that others may not see? What will it take for you to say what you see? When your perspective may be at great odds with others, how can you share, even at the risk of it not being received well? How can you stand more strongly in what you actually see and believe?

(6) Plus. Leading Beyond. In the LGBTQ community, it can be in vogue to make fun of how many letters we can add to our alphabet identity, e.g., LGBTQQI. And this is where we can begin to lead beyond. Intersectionality—how we integrate unique abilities and perspectives across identities—is a new frontier. Queer people cut across every ethnic identity. We have a unique ability to help build bridges to create even more innovation and greater value.

Coaching questions for the sixth phase may include: Who else can you partner with to bring greater value? What are unique perspectives that others are bringing to the table that you can see being complementary to your own?

Indeed, I am indebted to a senior managing director several levels above me in the hierarchy at the Wall Street firm Bear Stearns, where I worked, for reaching out to me and taking me under her wing. Her coaching helped me begin to take off that corporate drag that was weighing me down. In an assessment, she showed me how different—unique—I was from everyone else where I worked and how I could bring those special, more "artistic" gifts to my workplace. "We need what you have," she told me. With her assistance, I mustered the courage to go bold. In one notable instance, a PowerPoint presentation I gave included a dramatic representation of the solar system with the accompanying soundtrack from the 1960's hit musical Hair, "This is the dawning of the age of Aquarius." This was not your typical stockbroker presentation. But the metaphor and uplifting moment captured the attention of the traders and accelerated the rollout of a new project I was leading.

Inspired by that generous senior woman executive, I became a coach. What she gave me, I now pass on. What she told me; I now tell you: The world needs what you have. It's calling you. Do it.

References

1. How we work, AceUp, https://aceup.com/how-we-work/, Accessed 7/26,2021.
2. Isler, J.C., "The 'benefits' of black physics students." The New York Times. https://www.nytimes.com/2015/12/17/opinion/the-benefits-of-black-physics-students.html, 12/17/2015.

25

NO BARS, NO BINGO, THEN WHAT? GREY, GAY, BUT NOT YET IN DECAY

By Jerry Kajpust and Brian Gorman

"Getting old isn't easy by any standard, and it's much harder when you're more likely to be alone or have less income or not enjoy partner or spousal benefits, as many LGBTQ elders are."[1]

Research shows the number of LGBT adults above age sixty in the US is between 1.75 to 4 million and growing, as the aging baby boomer population creates a thriving elder population.[2] With today's U.S. life expectancy now at over eighty years, at age sixty-five there are close to twenty years of life yet to be lived at what was once thought to be old age and retirement. With this extension of healthy aging and life, we see new issues emerging. This is especially true for the LGBT community who experience a unique set of circumstances and issues that haven't before existed. LGBT people are living longer and are more open than in the past, though many often still carry with them the burdens, traumas and challenges from living in a pre-Stonewall era. We also have a generation that, as HIV/AIDS survivors, are living longer than many expected, with many who have lost friends during the AIDS pandemic.

Isolation is identified as one of the biggest challenges this generation faces.[3] A number of them came out of straight marriages after the kids were raised, have strained or lost family connections, or lack long-term partnering. Also, many more are single, living without the support of a "nuclear family" of children and/or grandchildren that their straight counterparts often have for support. Others face economic challenges as they are financially unprepared for a long life. Self-funded retirement plans and 401Ks generally weren't available in their early careers meaning that, if at all, financial planning began later in life leaving little investment planning for the future. Lesbians and people of color are more likely to live in poverty than white gay men. Older bisexual adults are more likely to experience greater social isolation and are more prone to depression. Transgender older adults are more likely than their peers to be forced back into the closet or forego needed healthcare.

We need to recognize the potential for this vibrant group that, as defined by Jane Fonda's TED talk,[4] are living "Life's third act." Many no longer identify with the young club/bar culture but aren't ready for a senior center either. So, what are the alternatives to bars and bingo? How do we effectively engage and empower this population? It's important first to not only identify their unique challenges but to also identify their unique skills.

Scenarios

What do baby boomer generation coaching clients have in common with issues around aging and what makes these issues unique for the LGBT population?

- Janet is seventy-one, single and needs to work. Aging issue: Janet struggles finding work as an older adult. LGBT overlay: Janet, married until she came out in her fifties, moved in with her partner and is now a widow. Janet has no retirement savings or pension and now faces the challenge of finding work with little marketable work experience.
- Joe is sixty-eight, lives in a major city and is looking for a place to retire. Aging issue: Find a good city for retirement with family for support. LBGT overlay: He is looking for a city where he can still be out yet afford to live comfortably. Joe, estranged from his family, does not have a retirement portfolio and sadly, has many friends who died during the AIDS pandemic.
- Bill is sixty-two, HIV+ and single. He is looking to be in a relationship again. Aging issue: Use family, friends or church/community groups as resources to find a spouse. LGBT overlay: He is no longer into the bar or online scene and has a narrowing circle of friends. He now wonders where to go to meet new people and possibly find a partner?
- Terry is seventy-five, and his partner, eighty. They can no longer live at home and need to move to an assisted living/retirement home. Aging Issue: Research retirement homes and assisted living options to move in as a married couple. LGBT overlay: Many retirement homes still don't allow same-sex couples in the

same facility to share living spaces and by moving into one may have to "go back into the closet" or live separately.

As you read through this chapter, keep these scenarios in mind, or more specifically, the clients you work with in your practice.

Attributes of a Generation

Through coaching, it is important to help clients identify and remember the many life experiences, challenges, obstacles, and successes they have already sustained and the personal strengths they have developed because of what they have lived through. There are many skills and abilities a person develops during their life, adaptability being a key one for this generation, and more specifically, resiliency and inner strength, when looking at the LGBT population.

Adaptability is a major theme across the boomer generation and applies on so many levels. Consider even one of the most basic experiences. For example, growing up as a child, phone calls were generally placed by a live operator, then the rotary phone took over, then onto the push button phone until mobile phones were invented, and now of course, smartphones have taken over. We can think about all of the changes and innovations that happened in careers, business, healthcare, social media, and in society in general for over the span of this generation with a list that can go on indefinitely. What is key to remember is how adaptable and flexible this population is when facing change. Through adaptation, this generation has met and exceeded these challenges by creating new opportunities and learning about what is new.

Resiliency is defined as the capacity to recover quickly from difficulties, toughness. Let's look at the issue of "coming out." Coming out these days can still be a challenge, though in many ways it's a rite of passage and there is a lot of support for young people claiming their identity. This was not the case for the elder LGBT population who were often pioneers, if they came out at all. Many have learned to accept their identity on a more personal level, remaining strong in spite of work or personal environments that did little to support or encourage them, and more often attacked, banned, arrested or fired them. They grew up in a time before social media when there was a lack of visibility, much less positive LGBT images or role models. In spite of the obstacles, persecution and even alienation, they have remained strong. This generation led the community in the battle for LGBT rights and acceptance, facing incredible obstacles and often persecution.

Inner Strength is something that is almost ingrained by now in people who have lived through so much, but this quality may not be easily recognized or acknowledged. "We made it through" or "That's just how life was, but I survived" are common statements though don't actually connect to the personal strength developed because of what has been experienced or endured. By exploring past successes and how these challenges were addressed and resolved, along with the significant changes that have been experienced, coaching can reveal an innate inner strength that is again necessary—and available—when facing current obstacles and when looking to achieve desired goals and results.

Coaching the Boomer Generation

How can coaches support their clients and provide the appropriate support they need for the challenges they face? Through the use of powerful questioning, clients can build self-awareness and begin to identify solutions and potential obstacles. This in turn translates into actionable steps and achievable goals resulting in desired outcomes.

Issue: Financial

Attribute: Adaptability. Help the client explore where they've made major or even minor changes in the past to adapt to new circumstances, cultures, values, challenges, etc. Explore what resources they sought out and used. Coach them to identify areas where they've made changes that have led to positive results.

Coaching: What financial resources do you have available? How important is it for you to secure additional financial support? Who do you have to be to ask for support? What resources can you find? What community resources may be available to support you financially?

Issue: Job/career

Attribute: Adaptability. Have the client look back on the various jobs they've done, explore volunteer experiences. Explore what they have learned and begin to translate these experiences into marketable job skills.

Coaching: What training can you take? What skills do you have? What have you done in the past that you can rebrand or reinvent for today? What makes your heart sing? What has to happen to turn that into a new career? What is holding you back?

Issue: Health/healthcare

Attribute: Resilience. As the old saying goes, "The mind may be willing but the flesh is weak." There is a slowing down of energy and physical acuity that happens in this aging population, but still a desire to participate and be active. Identify areas where the client is or isn't aware of health issues and physical well-being.

Coaching: What health issues have you faced and succeeded through in the past? What do you need to maintain a healthy lifestyle? Who is available to support you? What keeps you from accessing the healthcare you need?

Issue: Self-care

Attribute: Inner Strength. It is also important to focus on taking care of mind, body, spirit, and social support. Explore what the client currently does to take care of self, celebrate self, nurture self. Have them identify ways/things that can be added.

Coaching: Do you meditate? How do you treat yourself? How do you restore your (mental, physical, emotional, spiritual) energy? It's important to remember to bring in pampering when possible and however possible. What can you do in this area?

Issue: Retirement

Attributes: Adaptability, Resilience, Inner Strength. This is really the catch-all for everything and all these attributes can be explored to support this area. Issues can include loneliness, lack of family or social support, housing, financial resources, social connectedness, or any other area that presents with the client. Discover new ways to view current thinking and action.

Coaching: Where will you retire? What can you afford? Will you or have you considered any communal environments, and what challenges will that present? What will support your lifestyle? What do you require to support your needs? What arrangements do you need to put in place either for home care, retirement facility, and elder care? Who are the friends and family that are in place now? Who will be there in the future?

There is such rich potential for coaching both in terms of population size and providing support for achieving meaningful lives. In identifying a positive vision or future self for these clients, it's vital to remember their strong skills and vast experience. Through collaborative coaching, this group will be empowered to experience that dynamic "third act" of their lives.

References

1. Rhode, Jason. LGBTQ Seniors Face Unique Challenges, The Georgia Voice. May 1, 2018. https://thegavoice.com/community/features/lgbtq-seniors-face-unique-challenges.
2. Choi, Soon Kyu and Meyer, Ilan H, LGBT Aging, The Williams Institute UCLA School of Law. August 2016 https://www.lgbtagingcenter.org/resources/pdfs/LGBT_OAMarketResearch_Rpt.pdf.
3. Espinoza, Robert. Out and Visible. Sage. 2014 https://www.lgbtagingcenter.org/resources/pdfs/LGBT_OAMarketResearch_Rpt.pdf
4. Fonda, Jane. Life's third act. TEDxWomen. 2011 https://www.ted.com/talks/jane_fonda_life_s_third_act?

Resources

The Generations Project. https://www.thegenerationsproject.org
National Resource Center on LGBT Aging.
https://lgbtagingcenter.org
SAGE. https://www.sageusa.org.

26

THE UNIQUE DYNAMIC BETWEEN GAY MALE COACHES AND STRAIGHT FEMALE CLIENTS

By Noor Alexander

Gay male coaches have a unique positionality—in their general lack of sexual attraction to women—to be able to provide a healing container of safety, connection, understanding, and emotional intimacy for female clients that might not otherwise be possible if they had a different orientation.

Previous research findings have shown that, in opposite-sex [relationships], women are more likely to trust and confide in gay men than in straight men.[1,2,3,4] Russell and his colleagues have consistently found that this difference is linked to the absence of gay men's attraction and mating intentions toward women.[5]

The relationship of gay male coaches with straight female clients can provide a "corrective emotional experience" for women in relating to men. My personal journey of coming to embrace myself as a gay man and working through internalized oppression—including femme-shaming and internalized homo-aversion—has allowed me to expand my capacity to serve as an effective coach and ally to my straight female clients.

Similarities Between Gay Men and Straight Women

Gay men and heterosexual women have interesting commonalities that allow them to connect easily: they share an attraction to men, they both are "outside" groups, and they both have been injured by patriarchal culture.

Early on, as boys, gay men often receive messages like "toughen up," "don't cry," "don't be too sensitive," or "don't be a sissy." Gay men are taught to conform to heteronormative masculine standards to fit in and be accepted, often at a cost to their authentic expression and a sense of real belonging. Women are also socialized in a specific way that has costs to them, especially in the workforce. Given that women are generally not treated like men are in the working world in terms of equal consideration for advances, bonuses, and in terms of how sexual harassment cases are handled, it is interesting to examine the different coping mechanisms women use to navigate these inequities. Many of my female clients, have reported feeling a need to "harden" themselves at work and to compartmentalize their emotions (reserving feelings for their private life) in order to be taken "seriously" or to gain "respect" from male peers. It is interesting to note that the qualities of conventional heterosexual masculinity, such as toughness and pushing beyond limits, is the valued professional and cultural norm that the rest of us are expected to follow and subscribe to, however we may intrinsically depart from this inclination. One negative impact is a lack of space for diverse expressions and a lack of collaboration across different strengths.

Similar to women, as a gay man, my experience is that we are not treated or considered with equal consideration as straight men. Within heteronormative patriarchal socialization, both gay men and straight women are taught to separate from their softness and dampen their sensitivities in order to fit into a dominant masculine culture that privileges the qualities and needs of white cis-gendered heterosexual men over the unique needs and qualities of women and gay men.

Gay Men Coaching Heterosexual Women

As a gay male coach who has worked with many straight women, I have found that a special dynamic exists between gay male coaches and straight female clients and that they are well-suited to work with each other.

Using therapeutic language, first, the possibility for "sexual countertransference" from a gay male coach toward a female client is almost negligible; this means that that the gay male coach has an unlikely chance of being distracted by physical attraction toward the female client.

On a different note, it is very interesting to note that "Straight men, more often than women, report initiating opposite-sex friendships with the intent to gain sexual access to a woman they are sexually attracted to."[6] Given women's experience with this phenomenon, culturally, it makes sense that it would seem refreshing for heterosexual women to connect with gay men without having to navigate questions of potential interest and pursuit. As the literature states, "Gay men's lack of sexual motives toward women enhances women's willingness to trust and befriend gay men."[7] In addition, "Gay men's absence of deceptive mating-related intent contributes to women's perception of gay men's benevolence and honesty."[8]

Coming Out to Clients

While some gay male coaches may believe that disclosing sexual orientation is not relevant or essential, I have found it is useful and, in fact, additive in working with straight women. At the start of one professional coaching relationship, I remember a prospective female client taking a deep exhale after I revealed I was gay in the natural flow of our consult; it seemed like her body suddenly relaxed. She later shared with me that learning I was gay supported her to feel less guarded and more comfortable with me. She also shared that she ordinarily seeks out female practitioners, and discovering that I am gay helped her consider that maybe she could be understood by more than just women. Thus, for this particular client, my choice to share that I was gay helped her to open up and more fully to receive my support.

My experience is validated by research that finds the explicit knowledge of a man's sexual preference not only increased women's comfort with a gay man (vs. a straight man), but also affected the degree to which the women (particularly attractive ones) were willing to engage with a gay man at a more emotionally non-sexual intimate level…This increased engagement was mutual; gay men responded to the women's more intimate interaction behavior by displaying the same behaviors.[9]

This speaks to the kind of mutual connection and symbiotic relationship that exists between gay men and straight women.

Personal Narrative

My own lived experience as a gay man who has been injured by heteronormative patriarchal socialization supports me to have a particular vantage point and access to empathy that I draw on to support my female clients, especially around their pain points with men. For example, since I experienced being teased and bullied by straight boys for appearing gay and being different as a child, I can empathize with the experience of women who feel sensitive to domination and aggression by (straight) men in their lives. As gay men, many of us have received the implicit message early on from our socialization that being gay is somehow inferior, worthy of exclusion, and makes gay men "less of a man" (compared to straight men). This message is painful to bear. I long to live in a world in which the definition of "masculinity" and ideas of gender are broadened beyond narrow traditional bands and make space for various expressions, including seeing and valuing gay expressions as equal.

As such, I enjoy supporting women to identify and work through their own self-limiting beliefs about men that block them from stepping into their full power. Interestingly, some of my female clients have shared that they have experienced my gentle yet strong presence as a soothing counter-example to their experiences with other men, helping them expand their perceptions. Moreover, some of my long-term female clients who have had significant challenges with men in their lives, such as with exes or their fathers, have reported that our consistent, stable coaching relationship offered them healing in relating to men, allowing them to open up to possibilities again (like considering dating, which they had been closed to for a while). Thus, as old relational wounds with men began to heal, a new relational template for how to relate with men in a secure or healthy way can be created.

As a gay man committed to liberation, I aim to unpack and release the messages I have received from my male training to conceal my "softness," hide any trace of "femme," etc. The journey of honoring my authenticity and living by my own self-definition of masculinity—distinct from what traditional heteronormative masculinity teaches is the valued, golden standard—is ongoing, and, I find, requires rigor. As I am challenged in this regard, so too are women. Because patriarchal culture imprints that "hard" and "overly masculine" is aspirational, my experience with my female clients is that they also learn to mask or disown varying degrees of their softness and essential femininity in order to survive and fit into a straight man's world. This speaks to me of the tragic sacrifice of the feminine.

Through coaching, one way I work with this is to help my female clients to unpack their internalized patriarchy and guide them in exploring their native femininity and what it would look like to recover that essence, which some refer to as the "sacred feminine." This process may involve first mourning all that they perceive they've lost or given up in order to "fit in" or compensate for gender inequities. It may also look like exploring their divine feminine. I see my capacity to engage in this particular type of work and to hold fierce gay space as being a direct result of my personal work (which is ongoing) to confront and undo my own internalized gay and femme shaming.

This process really ignited for me in 2015 when I underwent a phase of drag immersion while living in the UK. That was when I discovered and became a huge fan of RuPaul's Drag Race (US)—a popular reality TV competition show in which US drag queens compete for the title of "America's Next Drag Super-Star." Though short-lived, this "drag period" in my life was very empowering and it allowed me to connect with different sides of myself that I had not previously tapped into. It was as if my feminine side, until then, had been a "Sleeping Beauty," lying dormant, awaiting the invitation to awaken. When I was in drag, I remember feeling things I hadn't felt before and it gave me permission to be and feel more self-assured, fierce, and free. Drag gave me permission to be daring, brave, powerful, and less self-conscious.

Interestingly, my then-partner remarked after witnessing me go through this transformation that he experienced me as integrating these qualities more in my natural self, outside of drag, as a result of doing drag. He experienced me as more confident. This reminds me of an impactful quote RuPaul says that his therapist shared with him many years ago that stuck with him, "The power you have in drag is available to you outside of drag." Similarly, it's almost like I learned how to be more of who I am because of drag; perhaps a more "complete" version of myself. I believe as we embrace more of our feminine colors, the more whole we all become (rather than less). This runs contrary to the given patriarchal cultural narrative.

My experience of doing drag was also eye-opening in terms of learning vicariously about male privilege and women's oppression. During my first night in full drag walking home alone in downtown Cambridge, England, I remember feeling vulnerable in a way I had not experienced before as a man (in non-drag). That night, as men stared at me in my full makeup, heels, and cute dress, I remember feeling uncomfortable with the objectifying gaze of onlookers. It was as if I suddenly understood male privilege in a way I hadn't before. I felt afraid of attracting unwanted attention, longing for safety and hoping to make my way home without harassment. This experience gave me a glimpse into the stress women may experience in public around receiving unwanted sexual advances from men. It helped me viscerally and somatically "get" in my body that needs, such as safety and protection, are significant and real for women in patriarchal societies. Thus, drag allowed me to have a small felt sense of women's oppression, which has supported me to expand in my empathy and compassion for them. The well-known quote from Emo Philips is to "Never judge someone until you've walked a mile in his shoes." My adaptation is "Never judge a gal until you've walked in her heels."

Conclusion

In closing, gay male coaches are well-matched to work with straight female clients. There is a distinctive quality to this configuration that is noteworthy. Research has shown that straight "women…can quickly develop close, trusting [relationships] with gay men."[10] This dynamic of safety as well as the potential for emotional intimacy and healing is connected to the gay male coach's lack of (or low potential for) physical attraction to the female client. I believe revealing our orientation as gay male coaches can be beneficial and provide value, rather than be a hindrance, for our female clients. It can provide comfort, safety, ease, and help them know how to orient toward us. My experiences as a gay man, including in drag, have allowed and shaped me to become a stronger, more available ally and coach to my straight female clients. For that, I am very grateful. As gay male coaches, we have the opportunity to be caring, non-threatening male presences for straight women, which can provide fertile grounds for transformation. And, in a small way, this can contribute to the healing of patriarchy in the world, which mustn't be underestimated.

References

1. Grigoriou, Tina. Friendship Between Gay Men and Heterosexual Women: An Interpretive Phenomenological

Analysis. London, England: London South Bank University, 2004.

2. Hopcke, R. H., & Rafaty, L. Straight Women, Gay Men: Absolutely Fabulous Friendships. Berkeley: Wildcat Canyon Press, 1999.
3. Muraco, A. 2006. "Intentional Families: Fictive Kin Ties Between Cross-gender, Different Sexual Orientation Friends." Journal of Marriage and Family, 68, pp. 1313–1325.
4. Russell, E. M., Ickes, W., & Ta, V. P. 2018. "Women Interact More Comfortably and Intimately With Gay Men—But Not Straight Men—After Learning Their Sexual Orientation." Psychological Science, 29(2), pp. 288–303 (p. 300 cited). DOI: https://doi.org/10.1177/0956797617733803.
5. Russell, E. M., Ickes, W., & Ta, V. P. 2018. "Women Interact More Comfortably and Intimately With Gay Men—But Not Straight Men…
6. Russell, E. M., Ickes, W., & Ta, V. P. 2018. "Women Interact More Comfortably and Intimately With Gay Men—But Not Straight Men…
7. Bleske-Rechek, A. L., & Buss, D. M. 2001. "Opposite-Sex Friendship: Sex Differences and Similarities in Initiation, Selection, and Dissolution." Personality and Social Psychology Bulletin, 27, pp. 1310–1323.
8. Russell, E. M., Ickes, W., & Ta, V. P. 2018. "Women Interact More Comfortably and Intimately With Gay Men—But Not Straight Men…
9. Russell, E. M., Ickes, W., & Ta, V. P. 2018. "Women Interact More Comfortably and Intimately With Gay Men—But Not Straight Men…
10. Russell, E. M., Ickes, W., & Ta, V. P. 2018. "Women Interact More Comfortably and Intimately With Gay Men—But Not Straight Men…

27

CHANGES AND CHALLENGES: FOUR GENERATIONS OF COMING OUT

By Patrick Boze and Garry Schleifer

We met at a Gay Coaches conference a few years ago, staying in touch and getting to know one another better. After sharing our "coming out" stories, we wanted to know more about coming out for other gay men. As coaches for gay men from a variety of generations, we knew it would be good to understand what experiences our clients may have and how they may vary by their ages. We wanted to see the similarities, differences, and progression of gay lives over many generations. We considered the "coming out" stories of four generations of men ranging in age from twenty to eighty. Two of the stories are ours. Altogether, they tell a story about coming out through many generations: what it was like, what has changed, and the work that still remains for gay men. We imagined that growing up in times when being gay is seen as more and more normal would make coming out easier. We found that things have changed dramatically, especially in the lives of the young men coming out today.

Like the rest of the men in this chapter, Harry, now eighty, began questioning his sexuality in his twenties while he was in a seminary to become a priest. He didn't understand what it meant to be gay. Sexuality was never discussed publicly and any conversation about sexuality was surrounded by shame. At the age of twenty-two during confession, he told the priest that he thought that he was gay and the priest said that because he was taking a vow of celibacy, his sexuality didn't matter. Later at the age of twenty-six, conflicted by his vocation and his sexuality, he left the seminary after eight years, with no tools to discuss his sexuality. It was a violent, fearful time to be a gay man, and even the police presence was a danger. There were no public role models, but he slowly integrated and eventually began to privately live as a gay man, but avoiding the conversation of his sexuality, mostly living as a straight man in public. He has long since came out and now, having survived the AIDS epidemic, serves as a surviving elder in our community.

For Garry, now sixty-three, coming out was what he considered "late" at age twenty-three. Leading a "straight" life was just what was done and expected. Being a tall white guy, it was fairly easy for him to blend into the straight world until he couldn't do it anymore. From an early age he knew he was different from the other boys, but didn't know what it meant or how to act on it. There were no role models for him. Somehow, he started to realize his difference was that he was gay. He started to explore his newfound sexuality. By that time, Garry was living away from home, building his career and life and free from any expectations or disappointment from his parents other than the regular "when are you going to find a nice girl and get married?" question.

His coming out was also right at the beginning of the AIDS pandemic. There were few public role models and they often had experienced hardship and struggle, like Larry Kramer, who died of AIDS, or Harvey Milk, who was assassinated. Anyone else who was "considered" gay was bullied and called out as sissy or gay. Sadly, due to his need to rush into everything gay, he was not careful and in 1987 contracted and was diagnosed with HIV. Luckily, Garry had the DNA to reject the expected deterioration and was not on medication until about twenty-five years later, when it was a one pill treatment. He is now undetectable.

For Patrick, now age forty, coming out at age eighteen was fraught with inner turmoil. In a society where homosexuality is a question of right versus wrong, being a gay man meant he was doing something bad. He was also told this at a young age by someone who molested him. He believed that if he told his family that he had been molested they would find out that he was gay and hate him. He began noticing that other people thought the same way, that being gay was wrong. This was certainly the opinion of a priest when Patrick casually asked him about homosexuality. So, he accepted it as true and felt horrible about himself.

He grew up believing he was not normal and thinking what a disappointment he would be for his parents. Then as a young man, watching the first season of Will & Grace, he saw his first role models of gay men living a somewhat normal life as out men. He had to make sense of both his traumatic experiences and this moral question of whether gay was wrong. Patrick's father also struggled with it but in the end, he chose his love for his son.

For Jacob, now twenty, a mentee of Patrick and fellow survivor of sexual abuse, coming out in high school was the norm. He found teachers, mentors and therapists with whom he could talk to figure things out. He also had thousands of gay men that he could look up to for examples of acceptance and belonging. He understands that sexuality is not a black or white issue and says that he's still figuring out his own sexuality, but he doesn't feel the need to identify himself as a gay man. When asked about his perception of the fight for equal rights for LGBTQ+ people, he said that while he understands that the fight is recent, he struggles to relate to it because, for him, it is distant history.

In his generation, for the most part, being gay is accepted, but he also grew up in a home with a father who had strong feelings against being homosexual. When he came out to his parents, he found his mother to be very accepting; however, his father did not provide his support and held onto his strong feelings that being gay was somehow wrong. That conversation continues.

We've found it interesting to compare these different experiences of coming out. Although there has been a steady change to acceptance, coming out is still an "event." Add into the mix the normal teenage coming of age physical and emotional issues, and perhaps a dose of lack of self-confidence and fear, and you have a recipe for concern.

At the Time of Coming Out	Harry	Garry	Patrick	Jacob
Role Models	No	No (very taboo and AIDS epidemic)	No (many had died from AIDS, still taboo)	Yes
Support from members of society (teachers, public officials, etc.)	No	No	No	Yes
Will & Grace was in my life	No	Well after I came out	Original	Reboot
Gay Marriage Legalized (in the US)	No	No	No	Yes
Laws Against Sodomy (in the US)	Yes	Yes	Yes	No

As we know all too well, our sexual orientation has its challenges. This can be clearly seen in other countries whose laws determine our very existence. Our own countries and communities do not provide 100 percent safety to be our own wonderful selves either. There are still stories of prejudice and hate bestowed upon us as we walk the streets of many "civilized" societies. As long as coming out is still a conversation that requires preparation, we will not walk with total pride and wonderfulness.

Our role as gay coaches, elders and men, is to continue to tell the good stories. To fight all the "isms" that hold us and our clients back from us being our fully expressed authentic selves. We need to keep spreading love and acceptance wherever we go and hold out a hand to those in need. Although things have changed a lot in the world, it still being fully accepted based on our sexual orientation has its challenges. We hope that one day "coming out" is a non-event, and that we can all support the progress we've seen in this larger story until we get there.

ABOUT OUR CONTRIBUTORS

We wish to thank our contributors and editors and all the various people who participated in this project. There are many reasons to be thankful and clearly the strong support from everyone helps makes this kind of project possible.

NOOR ALEXANDER: M.A., M.PHIL.

Noor Alexander helps his clients to finally create the life they've been waiting for so that they can experience profound aliveness from living a purpose-centered and soul-aligned life. His practice is aptly called "Aliveness Coaching." Noor holds two master's degrees, including one in Psychology and another in Cultural Anthropology from the University of Cambridge in England, as well as professional coach training from the Satvatove Institute. He is also an enthusiastic facilitator and practitioner of Nonviolent Communication (NVC).

To learn more about his services, please google "Aliveness Coaching" or email him at:
noor@alivenesscoaching.com.

MATTHEW BENNETT: BSC, MA, ACC

Matthew had a varied career in Education, taking him from teaching in England through development of international assessments, product management, sales, and finally consulting in South East Asia. He discovered coaching as a way of channeling his need to rescue people and subsequently developed a coaching practice based around people who are LGBT+, kinky or sex workers to become more integrated and successful in their lives and work.

PATRICK BOZE: MBA

Patrick is a New York State board certified, professional coach who offers private and confidential coaching and recovery services in a safe and therapeutic atmosphere. He's committed to his clients and serves them from a space of love and experience.

JOHN CARLSON: SPHR

John Carlson (he/him/his) is an HR and DEI expert and executive coach who has worked with some of the top organizations and leaders in the world, helping to analyze their business and create/revamp their D&I and culture programs. John has over ten years of experience in the people, talent, coaching, and D&I space. John calls Florida his home and resides there with his partner Michael and their Siamese fur babies.

Website: jdconsultsgroup.com
Email: john@jdconsultsgroup.com

HARRY FADDIS: D.D., CPCC

Life Coach, certified by CTI in the late 90s. Founding Member of The Easton Mountain Retreat Center (upstate NY), 2000 www.eastonmountain.org. Founding Member: The Gay Coaches Alliance: 2003; and the First Board President www.thegaycoaches.com. Life Coach and Spiritual Director, with a focus on men's issues: spirituality, eroticism, addictions, career, finances, personal power and leadership. Harry is also a painter and has practiced Tae Kwon Do since 2003, holding a 3rd Degree Black Belt.

DAMIAN GOLDVARG: PH.D., MCC

President | Goldvarg Consulting Group, Inc. Damian consulted for over twenty years to Fortune 100 companies, government agencies and non-profit corporations worldwide, in more than 40 countries. Being an expert in Leadership Development and in Personal and Organizational Effectiveness, he has worked with people from a wide array of business sectors such as technology, energy, finance, retail and manufacturing. He trains coaches, mentor coaches, and coach supervisors and is the Past President of the International Coach Federation (2013-2014).

BRIAN GORMAN: PCC

Coming of age during the civil rights movement, then attending college as anti-Vietnam war protests grew to claim a national voice, it isn't surprising that change took root in Brian early and has never let go. Through his business, TransformingLives.Coach, he serves clients who are facing major personal and professional transitions in their lives. He is a member of the International Coach Federation (ICF) and a Board member of the Gay Coaches Alliance. At TEDx Hartford, Brian spoke about his journey through change which began as a freshman at Syracuse University. Brian's business, TransformingLives.Coach, is a Certified LGBT Business Enterprise.

CRAIG HOWE: MBA, CPCC, PCC, ITCA

Through coaching, I seek to make the world fairer, kinder and more sustainable. Curiosity drives me. Having worked with over 500 executives, leaders and teams in more than 45 countries worldwide, I understand the value of difference. I believe the creative tension it brings leads to better outcomes. By inspiring clients to see differently and think big, this shifts what they imagine to be possible. I live with my partner and dog surrounded by fields and woodland in West Sussex. I am a keen photographer. I love to garden cook, hike, and explore the world in our VW camper.

JERRY KAJPUST: MA

As a professional business coach, I encourage and support exploration, examination, and action to foster sustainable results. I embrace the opportunity to inspire and empower others to take risks both professionally and personally to achieve their goals. Through powerful questioning, I support the exploration of ideas and concepts which are either unknown or as yet unexplored, leading to the potential for improvement. With more than twenty years of experience as a successful businessman and non-profit professional, I have extensive management and leadership experience across a diversity of industries and communities.

S. MARK KENNEDY: PH.D.

S. Mark Kennedy is a certified professional coach, adjunct professor at Widener University and shift leader at William Way Peer Counseling. Educated at Duke, Purdue, MIT Sloan and EB Theological Seminary, Mark held various technical leadership positions at DuPont for over thirty-two years where he created high-functioning global teams, drove effective culture change, and led organizations through M&A. Mark became well known for his team building and people engagement skills. His company, Sustainable Transformations LLC, provides individual, professional and leadership coaching, consulting, and transformational workshops with a focus on sustained transformational development and engagement.

BERNIE KETTLE: MA (CANTAB), CERTIFIED CONSCIOUS COACH, AND ACCREDITED JOURNEY PRACTITIONER

Bernie Kettle is dedicated to the world knowing the gift of gay men. He believes that gay men are destined to carry humanity into the future. That can only happen when we gay men are fully self-expressed and seen and celebrated for exactly who we are. Bernie mentors gay men who are ready to bring their gifts more fully into the world so that they can play their VITAL role in society. As greater numbers of gay men step into living boldly and authentically, together we will show the world the beautiful gift that gay men offer to humanity.

BRAD KRUEGER: MBA

Brad Krueger is a Business Success Coach with a passion for helping independent providers of professional services establish good business habits and make more thoughtful decisions. Over his twenty-plus year professional and entrepreneurial career, he has excelled at synthesizing abstract ideas into concrete outcomes that grow and strengthen the businesses he serves.

Brad has earned an MBA in Executive Leadership from the University of Wisconsin Madison and is pursuing Mental Fitness Coach Certification.

F. DOMINIC LONGO: PH.D., PCC

On his own journey into greater wholeness and thriving, Dominic Longo is devoted to catalyzing and cultivating the transformational journeys of other LGBTQ+ leaders. Founder of Flourishing Gays, Dominic is an executive coach, facilitator of transformation, and leadership development expert based in New York City.

A former Engagement Manager at McKinsey & Company and Professional Certified Coach, Dominic holds a Ph.D. in Arabic and Islamic Studies from Harvard University. A citizen of the United States and Italy, he grew up in Nebraska and is fluent in Arabic, French, and German.

JAMES LOPATA: MTS, PCC

James Lopata, VP of Coaching Supervision at AceUp, is an executive coach with over thirty years of corporate executive experience, including on Wall Street and in digital consulting. He's released two books on leadership and been widely published, including in Forbes, NPR, The Boston Globe, and The New York Times. He is a fellow at Harvard 's Institute of Coaching and serves as Board President of the Massachusetts LGBT Chamber of Commerce. He holds degrees from Miami University (Ohio) and Harvard University.

JEFF NALLY: MBA, PCC

Jeff Nally is an executive coach, coaching supervisor, professional speaker, and author creating no-nonsense neuroscience solutions with leaders to be more human at work. He is president of Nally Group Inc., a practice focused on the science of leadership. Jeff is Vice President, Global Coach Community at CoachSource where he engages and connects over 1,100 external coaches with corporate leaders. He is co-author of Rethinking Human Resources and Humans@Work. Jeff earned coaching certifications at Results Coaching Systems, The NeuroLeadership Institute, and supervision certification from Goldvarg Consulting Group. He is a Professional Certified Coach with the International Coach Federation.

RICK REDDINGTON: PCC

Rick Reddington is an International Coaching Federation Professional Certified Coach (ICF PCC) with MS degrees in Leadership, Positive Organizational Development and Human Relations. Rick completed his first coach training with CoachU in 2000 and was a Founding Member of Coachville; he remains committed to expanding the potential of professional coaching. Rick provides leadership development, professional presence, and career coaching, specializing with LGBTQ clients and those familiar with addiction and recovery principles. His professional background includes technology sales, value management, sales enablement, consulting, and organizational learning. Rick enjoys supporting professionals who are ready to grow with purpose and on purpose.

GARRY SCHLEIFER: PCC, CMC

A seasoned businessman bringing over thirty years of experience, Garry "walks the talk." His credentials draw from experience as the visionary behind several multimillion-dollar corporations as well as being the owner and publisher of choice, the magazine of professional coaching. (choice-online.com)

Garry comes from a place of "ruthless compassion" when helping his clients. He challenges them with transformative coaching, rigorous goals, an innate sensitivity, good humor, and non-judgment.

PETER SIMMONDS: PCC – EBC

Peter's career has focused on helping leaders and teams understand their purpose, identify their strengths and gaps, and navigate toward increased effectiveness. Peter has worked with leaders and teams in challenging, high-paced work environments where resources are limited, and expectations are high. In his executive coaching, Peter brings quick thinking, humor, and accountability to help leaders understand their cultural context, increase collaboration, more effectively navigate challenges, and balance the needs of their work and personal lives. He has built deep expertise across the 400-plus leadership sessions he has designed and delivered, focused on autonomy, self-awareness, team problem solving and human connection.

CATOR SPARKS: CPCC

Cator Sparks is a CTI trained Life Coach based in Charleston, South Carolina. While he is happy coaching a range of clients around the globe, his focus is on men and the queer community.

DAVID P WHITTLETON: MAOM, PCC

David is a performance-driven Life Coach and Leadership Consultant with eighteen-plus years of Senior Leadership experience at a Fortune 500 company and has a well-earned reputation and strong work ethic.

David has a Master of Arts in Organizational Management and a Bachelor of Science in Business Management from the University of Phoenix. He received his Professional Coach Certification and Energy Leadership Index – Master Practitioner credentials from the Institute for Professional Excellence in Coaching (iPEC) and his Foundations in Team Coaching Certification from the Global Team Coaching Institute (GTCI). He is currently studying for his Practitioner Certification from GTCI.

TONY V. ZAMPELLA: MSOL, CP

An educator, coach and consultant, who founded Bhavana Learning Group in 2000, Tony is working with clients to cultivate conscious leadership. Specializing in adult learning and leadership, Tony began coaching in 2000, and served as faculty at Mercy College until 2005. Other experiences involved LGBT/AIDS activism (1984-97), publishing a LGBT weekly newspaper (1986-94), and serving as a City Human Relations Commissioner (1993-97) for San Diego. A Zen Buddhist practitioner since 2000, Tony is certified in Contemplative Psychotherapy, Ontological Design, Open Space Technology, Appreciative Inquiry, Spiral Dynamics, and Spiritual Intelligence with degrees in Sociology (BA), Journalism (MS), and Organizational Leadership (MS).

EDITORS

THOMAS M. KEYDEL: M.S., M.ED

Thomas M. Keydel was educated at Bowdoin College, Northeastern University, and at Boston University. He has lived in the Boston area since 1981, working as a Certified Public Accountant, instructor, technical writer, small business entrepreneur, Life and Financial Coach, actor, playwright, and poet. He has one previous book of poetry and a longer work of non-fiction on the topic of decision-making. He is the principle of Creative Leap Coaching.

TIM KINCAID: EDD, PCC

Dr. Tim Kincaid is a leadership coach and consultant specializing in change management and leadership development. He is on several rosters of executive coaches with coaching companies and universities, and teaches college courses. Tim holds a Professional Certified Coach (PCC) credential through the International Coaching Federation (ICF), and is certified in several key personality assessments used in coaching. He served as president of both the ICF-North Texas chapter and the Gay Coaches Alliance. Tim and husband Larry live in Dallas/Fort Worth, Texas. His website is www.kincaidcoaching.com.

ADAM ROBERSMITH: MA, M. DIV, D.MIN

The Rev. Dr. Adam Robersmith is a spiritual director, Unitarian Universalist minister, scholar, and artist. Educated at Cornell University, Starr King School for the Ministry, Chicago Theological Seminary, and Fielding Graduate University, he has studied science, theology, history, human development, and the arts. The range of his interests and breadth of his education help him support the spiritual and religious lives of people with a wide variety of beliefs and practices. He also serves as a formation consultant for religious institutions. Online, he can be found at www.adamrobersmith.com. Offline, he can be found living and hiking in the woods of Connecticut with his partner.

Made in United States
North Haven, CT
27 July 2022

21887741R00104